CRACKER

Dedication:
For Mum & Dad

ACKNOWLEDGEMENTS:

I would like to express my appreciation to all those who have directly and indirectly helped me write this book. Without their knowledge, time, and support it could not have been written.

Special thanks are due to:-

Robbie Coltrane, Ian Stephen, Jimmy McGovern,
Russell Stockdale, Phil Fenerty, Sally Head, Gub Neal,
Paul Abbott, Catriona Mackenzie, Richard English,
Alex Benady, Rod Tootell, Jill Crace, Caroline Taylor-Thomas,
Adrian Sington, and Rod Green.

CRACKER

THE
TRUTH
BEHIND
THE
FICTION

JOHN CRACE

B⬛XTREE

First published in Great Britain in 1994 by Boxtree Limited, 21 Broadwall,
London SE1 9PL

This revised and updated edition published in Great Britain in 1995 by Boxtree
Limited

Text copyright © 1994 and © 1995 John Crace
Cracker copyright © Granada Television Ltd and Jimmy McGovern

10 9 8 7 6 5 4 3 2 1

ISBN 0 7522 0187 5

Printed and bound in Great Britain by
Cox & Wyman Ltd, Reading, Berkshire

A CIP catalogue entry for this book is available from the British Library

Cover photographs courtesy of Granada Television
Cover design by Shoot That Tiger

Inside photographs courtesy of Granada Television

Inside design by Design 23

CONTENTS

Preface To The New Edition   7

CHAPTER 1
FROM IDEA TO SCREEN   13

CHAPTER 2
THE WHOLE TRUTH   25

CHAPTER 3
BUILDING A BELIEVABLE BACKGROUND   41

CHAPTER 4
OFFENDER PROFILING   63

CHAPTER 5
THE IRRESISTIBLE RISE
OF THE SCREEN DETECTIVE   105

CHAPTER 6
CRACKER: THE STORY LINES   115

Preface
To The New Edition

WHEN THE FIRST few episodes of Cracker were shown two years ago they received massive critical acclaim, but the initial viewing figures hovered around the ten million mark. Not bad, but by no means a runaway success. Since then the series has gone from strength to strength. It has won 5 Baftas, including the viewers' award for best drama, 16 other international prizes, and viewing figures have soared to 15 million.

All this has been well-reported, but less obvious has been the impact that the programme has had on people's careers. Christopher Eccleston (DCI Bilborough), Robert Carlyle (the skinheaded Albie), Susan Lynch (the manipulative Tina), and Samantha Morton (Joanne the child abuse victim) have all gone on to have starring roles in television dram series this year - *Hearts and Minds*, *Hamish Macbeth*, *Dangerous Lady*, and *Band of Gold* respectively.

Nor are these the only four to do well out of *Cracker*. Robbie Coltrane has turned from star into superstar, and Lorcan Cranitch (DS Beck) recently played the leading role in the Screen 2 drama *Life After Life*. Geraldine Somerville (DS Penhaligon), who has risen from comparative unknown to Bafta nominee, is quick to acknowledge her debt to the programme. 'Cracker has made a substantial difference to my career. Not only has it given me a great deal more confidence in my abilities, it has also firmly established me in the minds of producers and casting directors as a good TV actress.' And the list goes on. With the sole exception of Graham Aggrey who played a black rapist in the last series - thereby highlighting the difficulties facing black actors - every single one of the Cracker villains has gone on to larger roles.

Success hasn't just been limited to those in front of camera. 'Like many writers, I always said yes to every interesting project that came along, because I knew that nine out of ten would come to nothing,' says Jimmy McGovern. 'After Cracker there was suddenly money available for nearly all of them' - including his screenplay for Priest which had been sitting on Michael Wearing's desk at the BBC for over a year. Michael Winterbottom, director of the first story, has gone on to direct Roddy Doyle's The Family, and Gub Neal, producer of the first series, has just taken over as Granada's Head of Drama.

While it would be surprising if there had been no knock-on benefits for those associated with such an acclaimed production, the scale of it has been breathtaking. Prime Suspect has been as big a success as Cracker, both with the critics and in the ratings, but who remembers anything other than Helen Mirren's portrayal of Jane Tennison? So what makes Cracker so special that even its minor characters can become household names?

Gail Stevens, the casting director for the first two series, deserves credit for talent spotting but, as she is the first to admit, it is Jimmy McGovern's writing that has been responsible for allowing the actors to show just how good they are. 'So many dramas simply focus on one central character, with all the lesser roles being little more than cardboard cut outs. If the writing for these parts is one dimensional then the acting will tend to be so also.' McGovern's achievement is to break the mould of the formula TV cop drama. As Susan Lynch says: "He doesn't write for a medium, he writes for real people.' Even the baddies are given a convincing explanation for the their behaviour; in most other series they are simply portrayed as either mad or greedy. If these were sufficient motivation for serious crimes Margaret Thatcher and Cedric Brown would be under almost constant suspicion.

McGovern himself is characteristically blunt about *Cracker's* Midas touch. 'When you make an intelligent well acted drama series that TV executives at the BBC and Channel 4 actually want to watch for their own enjoyment then you shouldn't be too surprised when your actors start popping up in all sorts of other programmes.

However strong the supporting roles may have been, a drama series stands or falls by its central character, and *Cracker's* reputation owes much to Robbie Coltraine's towering performance as Fitz. If you weren't crushed by his intelligence and wit, they you sure as hell would be by his size. While McGovern's writing was again critical, it needed someone special to convey both a sense of danger and vulnerability, and Coltrane's success can be measured by two successive Baftas for Best Actor.

Coltrane himself is in no doubt what he owes to *Cracker*. 'Fitz is the sort of role you dream about playing. He's such a complex character; unlike with other TV cops you're never sure just how pure his motives are. In the first series he con-

ducts a witch hunt on an innocent man and is partly responsible for sending him to jail, while in the second he has to live
with the knowledge that he may have incited a rapist to commit murder.' There are no easy answers in *Cracker*, the characters inhabit the same unforgiving world of confusion and
its consequences as its viewers.

Gub Neal believes that the excitement of working on
something new and challenging lifted everyone involved to
produce their finest work. When Neal was first asked to
come up with ideas for a new cop series, the brief was to find
another *Morse*. Thankfully he didn't bother. 'If you look at
Morse now,' he says, ' you can see it for what it is - a period
costume drama. Like many others I was sick to death with
these old familiar models of TV dramas, and I wanted to create something both substantial and heartfelt yet capable of
sending itself up. Thanks to everyone's enthusiasm and
inspiration, I think we achieved it.'

Whatever the reason for all the accolades, *Cracker* has
marked a watershed in TV drama, and is now the benchmark
against which all new cop series are judged. All almost all are
found wanting. Few can match it for the intelligence, pace,
and wit of the writing, for the quality of acting, and for the
high production values.

There is no doubt that success has fed on itself; merely
being seen to be connected with *Cracker* has done wonders
for all those involved. For Samantha Morton ' it has been the
launchpad for my adult acting career', whereas for others,
such as Chris Eccleston and Robert Carlyle, it has been the
ideal showcase to remind everyone of their talent. But it is
also true that the programme seems to have an energy and
creativity of its own that inspires everyone who works on it.

Make no mistake: come this October, Mark Lambert and
Brid Brennan - the two leading guest stars in the first story
of the new series - will be sitting by their phones with diaries
open.

Chapter 1

From Idea to Screen

INSIDE EVERY STRAIGHT police drama there's a maverick waiting to get out. Gub Neal, who became the producer of the first series of *Cracker*, came upon the idea of a forensic psychologist detective when he was working on possible story lines for a potential new crime series. 'We had seen a documentary about Professor Canter, the forensic psychologist, and we thought that it might just work to use a psychologist detective rather than a policeman. In the end, though, we decided against it. The introduction of a psychologist seemed too big an idea to fit comfortably into the story, and besides which, the way in which Professor Canter ground out his information on a computer screen didn't immediately suggest high drama.'

Nevertheless, the idea of a drama about forensic psychology remained at the back of Gub Neal's mind. He was convinced that a detective character using modern analytical techniques – a latter day Sherlock Holmes – would have immense appeal. When Sally Head, Granada's Head of Drama, put an edict out one morning in late 1991 requesting a dozen new ideas to be put before the commissioners before the end of the day, it resurfaced. A proposal was hurriedly drawn up which read:-

'A series of 2 hour dramas about a totally new-age detective.

Working class, but an academic; a self-made man who teaches in a university in the north of England. He's in his mid-forties, popular and well-liked by his students. He is, however, deeply resented by the police. His success at cracking cases they have found impossible is second to none.

How does he do it?

He's the first of a new breed. A criminal psychologist, making a science, and sometimes an art, out of studying criminal behaviour. Unlike the "intuition" of the detective's hunch, he uses anthropology, animal psychology, but mainly his own mind as a drawing board for penetrating crime. Brash, daring and sexy, he's a latter day alchemist with a 5K megabyte brain which he uses as a torch to peer into the murky depths of the human psyche.

The town marshall with a pocket full of Jung. He uncovers the mysteries behind the criminal mind. What makes a person put razor blades in baby food, or climb 30 flights of stairs to rape an old woman?

The question for this man starts not with *who* but *why*.'

This was hardly the most detailed of proposals, and indeed the Fitz that finally emerged was far less of the virtuoso polymath than was first envisioned, but it captured Sally Head's imagination, and she gave Gub Neal the go ahead to commission a pilot script.

The man that Gub had in mind for this was the Liverpool playwright and screenwriter, Jimmy McGovern. Jimmy had served his apprenticeship writing episodes of *Brookside*, had recently won the Samuel Beckett award for his blood and guts TV screenplay, *Needle*, and was currently working on a drama series for the BBC called *Priest*. 'Even though I was going through a really bad time with *Priest*, with my script lying on Michael Wearing's desk, I was reluctant to abandon it,' says Jimmy. 'So when Gub first approached me with *Cracker* I refused it, but he's a persistent man, and he came back to me again, and after a lot of thought I said "Yes" because I recognised its potential. I'd seen the *Silence of the Lambs* and had been taken by the idea of getting into the heart and soul of a killer through a man who knew about the dark side of life. '

Having found a script-writer, the next step was to cast the central character. Jimmy's initial thoughts were for a 'thin, wiry man with a sense of danger - a John Cassavetes type', and the first actor that Gub approached was Robert Lindsay. 'I'd been extremely impressed by his neurotic energy in *GBH*, and I was hoping he would bring that same element to Fitz.' At the time Robert Lindsay was having a great success with *Beckett*, was shortly to star as Cyrano de Bergerac, and was unwilling to take on a role that he felt might be too similar to the psychotic Derek Hatton figure in *GBH*.

Following Robert Lindsay's refusal, Sally Head and Gub realized that it was going to be difficult to get any major star to commit himself without having seen a script, and so Jimmy spent the whole of August finishing off the first draft. 'The story-line for the first two-parter, 'The Mad Woman in the Attic', was one that I had carried in my head ever since watching the Fugitive on TV as a child, when I had been struck by the idea of a dead woman, and a man found lying beside a railway track whom the police believe committed the murder but can't prove it.'

A script normally goes through two or three drafts before it gets shown around, but Jimmy had written with such passion and energy that Sally and Gub felt confident that they would be able to get someone to commit himself to Fitz on the strength of it. 'Jimmy's script felt as if it had wings.' says Sally. 'He had written with such intensity that we hardly needed to change a word.'

The person whom Sally and Gub now had in mind was Robbie Coltrane. 'Robbie had just done his first major straight acting role for a while as an ex-junky in *Alive and Kicking*, in which he had revealed a quality that we needed for Fitz. He was capable of presenting a character and asserting a presence that was genuinely dangerous. It's partly a physical thing - if he didn't like you he could hurt you - but he also has an intelligence that could abuse you. In fact he might well do so anyway, regardless of whether he liked you, just because he could.'

Jimmy was delighted that Robbie's name was in the frame, because he had become increasingly worried that he had created a character that no one would like. At the same time as writing the first draft, Jimmy had also written the following pen portrait of Fitz:-

His problem is he's easily bored.

He drinks heavily. He chain smokes. He gambles compulsively. All because he's bored. He chases women, but as soon as he's caught one, he's bored again. Why don't they just shut up and lie back and think of England? Why must they insist on conversation? So he attacks them. He attacks them because they're middle class and don't know what life is. He attacks them because they're working class and so parochial....

He's a criminal psychologist lecturing in a Northern University. He's probably the best in his field and he's got a string of publications to his name but fellow professionals think he's a maverick. That doesn't bother Fitz - they're just an bunch of boring old farts.

Fitz understands crime, you see. There's nothing immoral about it whatsoever. Crime is just big league gambling. At stake is your liberty; the prize could be millions of pounds or a wife six feet under - nothing to do with morality at all, just a simple calculation of risk and reward. That's the trouble, you see: no one is prepared to say things like that (bar Fitz). The whole world is living a lie and Fitz will tell you that he sees it as his duty to challenge the world, to expose lies and hypocrisy, to get to the core of what people really feel. But the truth's a bit different; Fitz takes on the world because he's bored.

Maybe it's all down to his Catholic upbringing. My God, how he hates the church. Those Jesuits taught him to think, yeah, and argue, but they really screwed him up in other ways. The Virgin Mary, for instance - the only woman he's ever really trusted. And then all that examination of conscience and analyzing motive. He's the world's leading expert on conscience and motive. Did you know, for instance, that nobody has ever, in the whole history of the world, done anything for a pure, decent motive? Quote Fitz an example and he'll destroy you. Soldiers laying down their lives for others? Only because they were too fucking terrified of being called a coward, too cowardly to be a coward. And conscience? *Schadenfreude* - well there you are. The bloody Krauts have got a word for it - for the way you laugh your balls off, when you hear that someone has fallen down a lift-shaft. But the English, the pious, anal-retentive English.... Hypocrites, all of them....

Fitz never stops. He just cannot stop. Occasionally a massive depression might strike - particularly just after he's lost a small fortune on a horse that should have won by half the track. When that happens, he'll drink and drink and listen to JJ Cale but eventually someone will say something (his wife for instance) and he'll be off again, defending, challenging....

He doesn't drive. When people ask him why he says it's because he's never been sober enough, but the truth is he's never trusted himself behind the wheel of a car - it's just too tempting to put your foot down and close your eyes and gamble that you won't hit anything before you've counted to twenty. So his main form of transport is taxi. But when he's skint (as he very often is) it's the bus. Now that's a problem for him because he just can't stand still so he's always walking to the next stop and then the next and, sure enough, that bus always comes racing along while he's between stops. And it's no smoking upstairs and down these days but he lights up anyway and, of course, someone protests and there's a row but these health fascists are all the same, the country's full of them...

So that's a little taste of Fitz - dynamic, charismatic, hurtling along the road to self-destruction....

As Jimmy himself would be the first to admit, this prototype Fitz was fairly rough and ready with more than a passing resemblance to Jimmy after a hard night, and Jimmy saw in Robbie an actor who was capable of making his creation come alive in a lovable way, without losing its edge. 'Even though Robbie has never compromised on the roles that he's taken, or maybe even because of it, he's always been held in great affection by his audience. With Robbie playing Fitz, people would be predisposed to liking him.'

Having read the script Robbie was enthusiastic about the part, but hadn't yet given a firm commitment, and Gub and Jimmy travelled to Glasgow ostensibly to 'discuss the part' but primarily to twist his arm. 'I was convinced that our meeting was going to be a disaster,' remembers Gub. 'Jimmy and I were both extremely nervous because we were desperate for Robbie to say 'yes', and Jimmy had started drinking well before lunch. By the time we sat down he was half-pissed and his first words to Robbie were, "I wrote the script and I want you to know that I see Fitz as a very thin man." I thought, "That's it, we're out of this restaurant." To Robbie's credit he hung on through lunch as Jimmy got drunker and drunker. I was willing Robbie to have a drink himself, but he stuck to Diet Coke which made me even more anxious and I drank too much myself. However, despite Jimmy's and my drunken ramblings, Robbie sensed that there was something in both Jimmy and the script to which he could respond, and he agreed to play Fitz.'

'Armed with the first two hour story and Robbie's commitment to Fitz, we submitted our proposal for five further hours of *Cracker* to Marcus Plantin, the Director of the ITV Network Centre,' says Sally Head. 'Although Marcus had only been in the job a short while he clearly liked what he saw, because he gave us the go-ahead on January 1.'

In order to write well for Robbie, Jimmy spent many hours talking to him about the things that made him tick and those parts of his personal biography he would be happy to incorporate into the role. Both men found they had a lot in common but even so, contrary to many reviews and gossip columns that speculated that Fitz was some kind of shorthand for Robbie, Fitz has always been much closer to Jimmy's alter-ego than Robbie's. Indeed, such was Jimmy's identification with Fitz that when he was writing the scene in the third story, *One Day a Lemming Will Fly* in which Fitz accuses Beck of having a moustache to disguise his homosexual tendencies, he found himself saying the same thing to a stranger at a party, and nearly got beaten up for his troubles.

It is true that there are some superficial similarities between Fitz and Robbie. Robbie smokes, has been known to swallow a dram or two, likes jazz and movies, but there is nothing terribly remarkable about any of that. Equally, there are some superficial differences. Robbie loves old cars, but Fitz is a complete Luddite, Robbie is what the experts call a 'smart gambler' - someone who can quit while he's ahead, while Fitz is the complete opposite - a 'degenerate gambler'.

On a deeper level, Robbie and Fitz share the same black sense of humour, which is something that is quite often found in people who have been affected by death, because it's one of the ways that people cope with it. The spate of Ayrton Senna jokes that emerged after his horrific crash at Imola say much more about his death's effect on a national psyche than any disrespect that might be implied towards the late Brazilian racing driver. Shakespeare understood this well with Hamlet making a string of terrible jokes on finding Yorick's skull, and it is something that Gub feels present day drama often misses. 'We tend to be rather po-faced and politically correct about death, but we wanted to redress the balance in *Cracker*. I worked on a number of episodes of *Casualty* and whenever there was an emergency, the doctors and nursing staff would become dreadfully serious. Having spent some time in an Accident and Emergency Ward, I know that a doctor would be far more likely to say: "Who won the footie?" or

"Look at the state of that."

Apart from an understanding of life's dark side, and the sense of humour that comes with it, there are many fundamental areas where Robbie and Fitz diverge, as Robbie himself points out. "I get a great deal of pleasure from the simple things in life. Last autumn I planted 200 bulbs in the garden because I wanted to see them coming up through the snow in the spring. Fitz would never bother with something like that. He's so intellectual, that he can't get any pleasure out of the predictable. Fitz is a cynic who spends his whole time quoting the price of things in the hope that he won't have to confront the value of them. Oscar Wilde once said that 'If you scratch a cynic, you'll find a bruised romantic' and so at heart Fitz is a passionate man, but he subconsciously pushes away everything he really wants. He yearns for a close family, but despises himself for wanting it, and wouldn't be seen dead doing anything that smacked of domesticity, whereas I'm at my happiest when I'm at home with my wife and son, putting up shelves with a Black & Decker.'

Filming started on the first story even as Jimmy was working on the last two. While the time-scale put him under a lot of pressure, it also gave him valuable insights into the other characters he had created. 'I had no real sense of what any of the coppers like Bilborough, Beck, and Penhaligon were like when I started writing. Once I saw the rushes from the first story, they began to come alive for me. I could see what the actors were good at, and I tried to write to their strengths.'

However strong the acting, though, any drama ultimately stands or falls on the quality of the story and the writing, and Jimmy was acutely aware of this. 'The best stories are those where the killers have such a good reason to kill that even if the viewers can't condone their behaviour, they can at least understand them and care about them. I used to love the TV series *No Hiding Place* for just this reason, because I would often find myself almost willing the thieves or the murderer to get away with it. I tried to do the same with *Cracker*. I can identify with Sean and Tina in the second story, *To Say I Love You*, and I can understand the urge to kill the beast within which is at the heart of everyone's desire to find Cassidy guilty of killing the young boy in *One Day a Lemming Will Fly*.'

Jimmy immersed himself in the writing, and often found that he had over-written each episode by as much as twenty minutes. He still feels sad that some scenes were left on the cutting room floor, especially one in *To Say I Love You* when Fitz stands with his eyes closed in Penhaligon's flat, and predicts exactly what will be there, down to the copy of *She* magazine - except for one thing, her drum kit, her one symbol of non-conformism. Whatever regrets Jimmy may have though, the net result was tight, fast-moving, emotionally direct scripts to which the cast and production team could respond.

'We realized that there was a huge hunger for intelligent drama,' says Robbie, 'and we were all committed to making something a bit different. We all need a dose of feel-good escapism like *The Darling Buds of May* from time to time, but we felt that too many TV programmes patronise their audience. So many police dramas are one-dimensional whodunits with a denouement at the end. In *Cracker* the interest isn't who, because the viewer often already knows, but why and it makes people think about their own prejudices and fears. We all have some experience of sexism, racism, homophobia, and religious persecution; we all have fears about loved ones dying, and so why should they not be challenged and explored on prime time TV? It's not just the middle-class intellectuals who are capable of understanding and accepting difficult, unpalatable ideas.'

Gub makes the point more forcefully still. 'You hear a lot of talk about 9 o'clock watersheds and what is and isn't acceptable, but the truth is that more often than not the rules aren't imposed by censors but by programme makers worrying about what the viewers might think. One of the rules of Morse was that the camera never went into the autopsy room. This was nothing to do with censorship, and everything to do with making the violence wholesome, and giving the audience the impression that a murder was just a jigsaw puzzle to be solved. In Cracker I deliberately set out to hire people who shared my desire to show no respect for the false boundaries that existed. There can be nothing more arrogant than presuming to know what other people want, and so we set out to make a programme that we ourselves would want to watch. We were sick to death of stereotypes. In most cop dramas there are good cops and bad cops, but the truth is that they are all a mixture of both. Jimmy's scripts showed this and inspired everyone.'

'Gub and I took great care over our choice of the director of the first story,' says Sally Head. 'We drew up an A list of directors and were delighted that we could get Michael Winterbottom, who had a great success with *Under the Sun* to work with us. We felt that whoever we chose would set the tone for the rest of the series, and we rightly thought that Michael would be able to get across the gentler, more human qualities of Fitz, without diluting the uncompromising nature of the drama.'

That Sally, Gub, Jimmy, and Robbie were right to put their faith in *Cracker* is proved by audience ratings of well over 10 million viewers and a clutch of BAFTA awards. The sketchy character, at first abandoned in the belief that the work of a forensic psychologist was too boring to sustain a drama series, had been transformed into one of the most unique and compelling characters ever seen on television.

CHAPTER 2

THE WHOLE TRUTH

THERE ARE SMALL truths and there are big truths, and *Cracker's* prime concern was with the big ones, as Jimmy McGovern explains. 'We had a lot of people hammering the series over its handling of police procedure, which is fair enough, as I'm sure that the rules of P.A.C.E. (Police and Criminal Evidence Act) wouldn't allow Fitz to have done all sorts of things that he actually did. But the format we chose gave us much more scope to examine bigger ideas like 'what men feel like doing to women' which are fundamentally much more interesting. Human emotions are a universal currency, and it is absurd to imagine that any feeling you've felt, however perverse, hasn't been felt by many other people. I was once talking to a group of people about how when I was waiting to make my confession as a child I often felt as though my sins were so bad that the person standing behind me could see them imprinted on the back of my head. It had never occurred to me that anyone else could have felt like this, but one woman out of the 20 in the group admitted she had experienced exactly the same feeling.

'We didn't want to get so hidebound by correct procedure that we weren't free to examine the wider truths of these emotions. I'm sure the official police line on murder is that they would be delighted if they never had to deal with another one, but in their heart of hearts I bet some coppers must get sick to death of dealing with routine burglaries, and can't wait to get stuck into a nice juicy murder.'

Given these parameters, *Cracker* was never going to fall into the *Prime Suspect* mould which set its store by attention to police detail, but by the same token, Gub Neal took sufficient notice of procedure to ensure that there was nothing in the scripts that went totally beyond the bounds of possibility. 'The advantage of doing this is that it creates a bridge between what the audience knows and the drama, so that the story never becomes incomprehensible,' says Gub. 'There are a number of incidents in all three stories that are somewhat far-fetched, but then you could say the same about Greek tragedy or a Stephen Spielberg film. Good fiction must be believable, but with a suspension of disbelief. The desire for procedural correctness mustn't deny the poetic interpretation of characters as people.

'We originally considered ending the third story, *One Day a Lemming Will Fly*, with Bilborough calling off the press conference. Correct procedure would certainly dictate that this is what a police officer should do, but given Bilborough's psychological make-up and his relationship with Fitz, it would have been out of character for him to have done so. Neither of them inhabited a forgiving world, and to have had a happy ending would have been a complete *volte face*. That we had adopted the right approach was confirmed for me when Jacky Malton, the senior woman police officer who advised on *Prime Suspect*, said that although the way things happened in *Cracker* were sometimes highly improbable, the relationships between the police were in many ways much more credible than in had been in *Prime Suspect*.'

The man to whom Jimmy, Gub, and indeed Paul Abbott, the producer of the second series, turned for procedural advice was a retired police officer called Philip Fenerty. Phil had joined the Lancashire constabulary in 1949, serving mainly in the CID. In 1971 he transferred to run CID at Heathrow airport, and for the three years up till his retirement in 1979 he served as the Liaison Officer for the Police Scientific Development Branch at Sandridge near St Albans, where he was responsible both for finding out what equipment police forces wanted and for making them aware of what was available. While Phil was stationed at Sandridge he was approached by a friend working for Central TV who wanted some help with various stories for *The Sweeney*. 'I gave him a few procedural tips and an idea for a clash between a graduate on accelerated promotion and an old sweat detective sergeant. He was delighted with this and offered me some cash which I declined. What I did say though was: "Bear me in mind when I retire".'

Upon leaving the force Phil became a full-time police consultant. He read books and kept in touch with old colleagues in the Home Office and the police to keep abreast of developments in the legal system, and was employed as a consultant to all sorts of programmes from *Morse*, *Saracen*, and *Prime Suspect*, to various full-length feature films. Given Phil's involvement with *Prime Suspect*, he was a logical choice for *Cracker*. 'The deal that I always make is that I will point out all the procedural errors in the script, but it's up to the producer whether he chooses to act on them,' says Phil. 'After all, if I was going to be offended when my advice was ignored,

I'd have stopped working on *Cracker* a long time ago. Generally speaking, much of the procedure in the series is a compromise between what Jimmy and I would like to see happen, with the solution being just about within the bounds of plausibility.

'The very first draft of *Cracker* that I was given bore little resemblance to the final version. It was wild, and certainly gave me a few concerns for Jimmy's mental health. It was like an extreme version of *Starsky and Hutch*. After the woman's body had been found on the train, Jimmy had her body being carried up a railway embankment to an ambulance, rather than just being left on the train and carried to the next stop. Likewise, his directions for the police search of the train read: "Busy, busy, ripping everything and wrecking the train", when in real life the search would be slow and methodical. My other point about this opening sequence got ignored. If a body is found on a train it is the British Transport Police (BTP) who are called in, not the local CID. The BTP aren't just gate-openers, and it's a bit of an insult to suggest that they can't handle a death. CID would only get called in much later if the BTP were having no joy with their investigation.'

The rules of PACE would never allow a psychologist to interview a suspect, other than to determine if he or she was fit to be questioned, before he or she had confessed. However, since some of the strongest scenes in *Cracker* are when Fitz confronts a suspect, Phil found that a lot of his work was thinking up ways, however unlikely, to make this happen. 'In the original draft for the first story, *A Mad Woman in the Attic*, the amnesiac monk was kept in police custody for days at a time. I pointed out that the rules of PACE do not allow the police to hold a suspect for more than

36 hours without charging him. I suggested that the way round this was for the amnesiac to voluntarily surrender himself to Fitz's medical supervision. Even then I had to keep my eyes open, because in the scene where Fitz and the suspect travel down on the train to meet a woman who claims to be his wife, the original script had a couple of police officers accompanying them - which would have indicated that the suspect was back in police custody.'

There were some scenes where Phil's advice was completely disregarded. 'There was nothing wrong with having Fitz turn up with Penhaligon at the alley where the loan shark has been murdered in *To Say I Love You* but no police officer would ever have allowed him to roam around trampling over the evidence. A policeman's first duty is always to preserve the scene of crime. Even when senior officers turned up because it was a high profile crime and the press were out in force, I would never allow them to go inside the area to be taped off.' However, there was one scene about which Phil felt so strongly that he told the producer that if it was decided to keep it and someone objected, then he would want it publicly acknowledged that he had advised against its inclusion. 'It was in *The Mad Woman in the Attic* story. The script called for DS Beck to be seen putting on a rubber glove, saying to the suspect: "I'm going to conduct an internal search", to be followed, moments later, by loud screams coming from the police cell. This was nothing more than torture, and it just doesn't happen. If anyone's going to do an internal examination, it's the police surgeon. I'm not being naive about this. I've seen policemen lose their temper with suspects, and I know that the odd punch does get thrown, but their colleagues, junior officers even, will always try and pull them off.

Anyone who wants to interrogate a suspect has to get clearance from the custody sergeant to do so, and no custody sergeant would allow Beck to get away with torture because his job would be on the line if he did. The only way it could possibly happen was if the whole police station was in on a cover-up, and that would mean that everyone from the most senior ranks downward was corrupt. This isn't completely unknown, of course, but a random act of torture just couldn't occur in a police station that had straight officers like Bilborough and Penhaligon.'

This scene was later changed, partly due to Phil's recommendation and partly to improve the dramatic effect. When it was finally filmed, an atmosphere of menace was created when Beck simply threatened to find an excuse to conduct an internal search.

In general, though, Phil is quite happy with the way the police come across. 'There are various small things I would change, like DCI Bilborough calling DS Beck by his christian name when he's giving him a dressing-down. A senior officer would never be that matey when he's giving one of his men a bollocking. In fact, the first thing Bilborough would do is to emphasise the difference between their ranks by calling Beck "Sergeant". Otherwise, though, Bilborough is a thoroughly credible character. I would like to believe that an officer like him would have had the guts to call off the press conference, at least until he's had time to evaluate the evidence, in *One Day a Lemming Will Fly* when Fitz tells him that Cassidy is innocent, but I can think of one or two officers that I came across in my career who wouldn't have done so either.

'DS Beck is a little harder to take, but that's not just because he's a bit of a bully and a sadist. The police force makes a point of trying to recruit from a wide cross-section of the community, and if you adopt such a policy you must expect one or two weirdos to slip through the net. However, once an officer like Beck had shown himself in his true colours, I would expect him to be jumped on hard, and I don't think he could have made it to sergeant without being found out. He might get away with being too aggressive to a suspect once or twice, but he would be found out soon afterwards. It's not that his colleagues would necessarily report him immediately, but they might well ask to be transferred away from his shift. Once a senior officer starts getting these sorts of requests, he soon wants to know why.

'DS Penhaligon is the best character of them all, and she reminds me very much of a woman police officer who once worked for me. She was a qualified quantity surveyor who decided to jack it in and join the police, and she was the most reliable officer in the station. If you asked her to do something, you could guarantee that it would be done properly. Penhaligon is just like that. She wants to show that she's as good as, if not better than, the male officers, and she's prepared to put in the extra 10% effort to prove it. She's not quite as relaxed or flexible as the male officers, but that is again authentic. Many WPCs are worried that members of the public don't take them as seriously as their male colleagues, and so they often do things very much by the book. If I was Penhaligon's boss I would be delighted to have her on my team, though I would worry about her involvement with Fitz.'

Collaborations between the police and psychologists were not standard practice when Phil was a serving officer, and so he had no first hand experience of this. In order to offer useful advice, Phil canvassed the opinions of various policemen. 'The younger policemen had a guarded enthusiasm for psychologists,' said Phil, 'but the general response was one of indifference. Perhaps their reaction was partially prompted by none of them having had a rip-roaring success with a psychologist, and most police would lump them in with psychics and other well-meaning types into the "I'll try anything once category". During the Moors murders enquiries we would get all sorts of people phoning up to say they had dreamt that a body was in a certain location, and we would always follow these reports up, because when you're desperate you'll do anything. However the more normal police response to enquiries that are going nowhere is to start again from the beginning rather than to call in an outsider. You re-check statements and house to house enquiries, because policemen are just as liable to be lazy as anyone else. Sometimes policemen can't be bothered to go back to a house a third or fourth time to make sure he's interviewed every person living there. On one enquiry I was involved with we found that a police officer had ticked off houses as visited that had been demolished years ago.'

One thing that all the police Phil spoke to were agreed on was that they wouldn't use a psychologist like Fitz, or if they did, they would make damned sure they only did so once. As a result, Phil tried to get Fitz toned down a little. 'No police chief would allow a wild cannon like Fitz to have the freedom of the police station in the way he does because he certainly wouldn't want to run the risk of him upsetting your policemen and women. It would be far more likely that Fitz would be provided with whatever information he wanted and left to get on with it by himself at home or in his office. I think I managed to persuade Gub to ease off on some of Fitz's more excessive rudeness to junior officers, but he still offends the policeman in me. Personally speaking, I would love Fitz to get it hopelessly, disastrously wrong and commit suicide, but my 26-year-old daughter thinks he's absolutely bloody marvellous, so there's no accounting for taste.'

If it is the police's job to put a suspect in the frame, it is the forensic scientist's job to provide the corroborative evidence to substantiate or refute the charge. The forensic scientist often gets little more than a passing mention in TV dramas even though he is an integral part of the investigative process, as the action tends to focus on the more glamorous side of detective work, but there are few TV scriptwriters and editors who don't make sure that their forensic evidence is accurate, and those on *Cracker* were no exception. The man to whom the scripts were sent was Russell Stockdale.

Russell had joined the Home Office Forensic Science Service in 1970, where for 16 years he investigated crimes on behalf of the police. In 1986 he left to join Forensic Access, a private practice mostly concerned with defence work which had been established eighteen months previously by Dr Angela Gallop, a former colleague at the Home Office. 'We had both become very aware that the Crown held all the forensic cards and that the defence was poorly served as far as high quality advice was concerned,' says Russell. 'We wanted to redress that balance to ensure that if a defendant was found guilty, it was only after the evidence had been tested and proven in court, and not because his lawyer had failed to verify or understand the significance of the evidence.'

So what does a forensic scientist do? 'We specialize in murder, rape, and mayhem,' says Russell. 'Our job is to examine the biological evidence, the blood, saliva, semen, hair, nail clippings, and textile fibres - we haven't trained to do DNA testing - and to place it in the context of the incident. This last point is vital; just because something is exactly what the police suggest it is, does not mean that there cannot be an innocent explanation for how it came to be found where it was. In one case I was advising the defence in an alleged rape and I was sent some dried semen that had been found in the woman's bed. I checked the police findings and it was indeed the suspect's semen, but I could find no traces of vaginal fluid mixed with it. I then noticed that in the police reports it was confirmed that the suspect had been sleeping in the victim's bed for fourteen days prior to the incident. So the evidence was exactly what the police claimed, but it was meaningless in relation to the charge, and the prosecution abandoned the case.

'This was a more unusual example, but the more common problem you have to be aware of is when a policeman goes straight from the scene of a crime to arrest a suspect, thereby running the risk of contaminating some evidence. The sort of thing that can happen is that the police can go to a reported rape and collect the victim to take her to the police station. The same car might then be sent out to arrest a suspect, and if the forensic evidence depends on microscopic textile fibres to link the man to the crime there is no way of determining whether they got there innocently when he was picked up, or during the assault.

'Working for the defence, you have to take a lot on trust because you only get the evidence once the police have a suspect and their forensic scientists have examined it, and so it is as well to be wary. I've been sent photos of a scene of crime in order to understand where a piece of evidence was found and been assured that they depict the scene as it was found, and yet items of furniture were in different positions in different photos.'

'Often I will agree with the police scientist's findings but disagree over interpretation, but sometimes I will even discover evidence that the prosecution scientist has missed. I was advising the defence of a man who was accused of rape at the Henley regatta. The woman's version of events was that this man had forced her to have sex by ripping open her dress, pushing her to the ground, and throwing himself on top of her. The defendant's version was that the girl consented to sex and sat astride him. I was sent the man's trousers which the police scientist had noted were covered with "what looked like soil staining" on the front. If this was correct, it would indicate the defendant was lying. I asked to see the girl's dress which for some reason had escaped police examination. Not only did I find that there was no sign of ripping, but there was the same look-alike soil staining on the inside of the dress. I surmised that this was in fact fake body tan which had come off, which given the defendant's stains on the front of his legs would suggest he had been telling the truth. I'm happy to say the defendant was found not guilty.'

As a sideline to his more important work, Russell also acts as a consultant to TV police series. He worked on all three *Prime Suspects* - 'there were the usual problems of pathologists doing forensic scientists' work and vice versa, and they had got the time-scale for a blood grouping test all wrong' - and like Phil Fenerty, he was the logical choice for *Cracker*. Some of Russell's work was concerned with attention to detail. 'In

Mad Woman in the Attic they wanted to know the direction and power of an arterial spray, so that the blood would be in all the right places on the walls and ceiling when the girl was found with her throat cut on the train. I was also pleased to note that they had the forensic scientist in the correct uniform for the job (white overalls), though I was horrified that they were covered in blood. No professional scientist would leave a job looking like he had been working in an abattoir.'

In the new series, Russell has advised on knife wounds - 'they had the blade going through the organs in the wrong order' - but much of his advice has wider implications than might first appear. In *Mad Woman in the Attic* Jimmy came up with the idea of there being two different razors involved in the murder to give the story an extra dimension, and Catriona McKenzie, the script editor, called Russell to see if this was at all plausible in a crime of this nature. His reply that it was, since the first razor would most probably have been blunted on the bones of the girl's fingers as she resisted the attack, thereby making it unlikely that he could have shaved her pubic hair after her death without cutting her, may seem like a minor detail but it gave the go-ahead to this part of the story.

There is something quite fitting about this, because when a body is found in suspicious circumstances it is the forensic scientist, not the police, who decides whether a crime has been committed. Of course, when a woman is found with her throat cut as in *Mad Woman in the Attic*, or a man is found dead in an alley or on waste ground as in *To Say I Love You*, a policeman wouldn't have to be Einstein to work out that a crime had been committed, but he would still have to await the forensic scientist's confirmation. Sometimes, though, the situation is far less clear cut. Russell Stockdale was called in to investigate a case in Sheffield where a putrefying body was found in an abandoned house that had been partially ransacked. 'The body was badly decomposed and there were no visible injuries which meant that the pathologist was unable to determine a cause of death. There had clearly been a burglary but no one was certain whether the man had died of natural causes prior to it, or whether he had been killed during the break-in. Two things struck me about the case; all the downstairs rooms had been ransacked but half the upstairs rooms were untouched and the body, which was lying on the upstairs landing, looked alright from the back as you came up the stairs, but truly horrific from the front. The rooms that had been burgled upstairs were on the horrific side of the body, and it crossed my mind that if someone was robbing the house at night he would start downstairs and work his way upstairs. He might then have caught sight of the body from the back in his torchlight as he went upstairs and thinking that it was a tramp sleeping off a hangover, stepped over him to go through two of the upstairs rooms. It would only have been when he went to step back over the body to ransack the other rooms, that he would have seen it from the front, and at this point he could have been so traumatised that he fled in panic without finishing the job. There was something that was unidentifiable but looked as though it might have been a footprint in the brains of the body that had oozed across the landing, which tended to back up my thesis, and when I mentioned it to the police they were quite happy to accept my version and the enquiry was wound up.'

In order to determine whether a crime has been committed or not, the forensic scientist needs the scene of the crime to be preserved as accurately as possible. This did not happen when the loan shark was found battered in the alley in *To Say I Love You*. The scene was properly sealed to prevent onlookers getting too close, and the body had been examined and covered, but Fitz was allowed to roam around before all the evidence had been collected. It's not that it's inconceivable that he would be there, but he would have certainly got a severe ticking off for kicking at a pile of bricks from which he was saying the murder weapon was taken. Likewise, a forensic scientist would have had a heart attack if he had known that Fitz, Bilborough, Giggs, and Penhaligon had staged a reconstruction before the walls had been checked for human hair and fibres.

In the context of the drama this was a small point, and many crime scenes are less than satisfactory as far as forensic evidence goes, but the perfect scene does exist, as Russell recalls: 'A body had been found on wasteland in Newcastle. The police had followed the footsteps of the man who found the body to inspect the scene, and then withdrew the same way and then sealed off the area. Myself and the police surgeon arrived at the scene at the same time and we discussed what we each needed to do first before crossing the cordon. We then took the same route to the body and the surgeon determined that it was indeed dead. I taped all exposed areas of the body, both clothed and unclothed, so that they could be analyzed for any traces an assailant might have left behind. The body was then turned over, and the taping process repeated. It was then taken to the mortuary where the clothes were taken off, with each item separately bagged and sealed, and samples of hair and nail clippings were taken.'

Forensic psychologists, like Fitz, are usually only called in once a link between certain crimes has been established. The responsibility for this generally falls to the forensic scientist, and it is one of the most difficult things he can be called upon to do. 'I was based at Bradford for 6 months to work on the 'Yorkshire Ripper' enquiry,' says Russell. 'There had been about six or seven victims already by the time I became involved, and we were desperate to come up with some results. Whenever a new body was found, it was always a problem to know whether to link it to the 'Ripper' or to put it down to a copy-cat, because unfortunately once the number of victims mounts up details of the crime begin to leak out, and you do get imitations. So, we were under pressure from the start: if we failed to link the crimes we might lose valuable evidence, and if we linked them wrongly we could throw the enquiry right out.

'We came up with a set of guidelines, criteria to be met, by which we felt we could confidently link a victim to the 'Ripper', but it wasn't infallible. When Yvonne Pearson was found half-hidden under a burnt out sofa on scrub-land I argued that she was a 'Ripper' victim since one of his traits was to return to a body and move it into the open if it hadn't been found. I felt that the way that her trousers hung suggested that they had been undone and then done up again some time after death, which would indicate that her murderer had revisited the body. Neither the police nor my colleagues agreed with me, and the Yvonne Pearson case remained open until the 'Ripper' was caught and confessed to it.

'There was a further murder in a Lancashire garage which remains a matter of speculation because the 'Ripper' never admitted to it, but it gives you an idea of how difficult linking can be when you only really have modus operandi to go on. The police were criticised for being misled by the 'Ripper' tape which turned out to be a fake, but we couldn't afford not to take it seriously. At one stage in the investigation we had two boards pinned up at the enquiry headquarters, one for what we definitely knew about the 'Ripper', and the other for what we thought we knew. The latter was almost full, but the former was virtually empty. Indeed when the 'Ripper' was eventually caught it transpired that he had already been interviewed three times and released.'

Fitz solves crime through a mixture of intuition and emotional intensity. In *Mad Woman in the Attic* he almost forces the suspect suffering from amnesia to remember what happened, thereby pointing the investigation to one of two other men on the train. In *To Say I Love You* Fitz turns the tables on Tina, who has gone into the pub to lure him to his death, by recognising, through insight and intelligence, that she is Sean's partner and he has her arrested by Penhaligon. In *One Day a Lemming Will Fly* he finally acknowledges that Cassidy isn't the young boy's killer when he hears what he understands to be the emotional truth of the story. Real life isn't quite like this, though. Intuition can play a part in an enquiry, but it is forensic science that provides the evidential framework. After all, Fitz may get his man, but it is the forensic evidence that will convict him.

CHAPTER 3

BUILDING A
BELIEVABLE BACKGROUND

WHEN ROBBIE COLTRANE agreed to play Fitz he realized that there were two areas he was going to have to research to give a convincing performance: gambling and forensic psychology. The gambling was relatively straightforward. 'I spent a day with the manageress of a Manchester casino who explained everything to me, from the nuts and bolts of blackjack and roulette to the psychology 'of winning and losing,' says Robbie. 'I am the sort of bloke who can walk into a casino and leave when I'm ahead, and so, although I can see that gambling can be an addiction, I've never really understood the compulsion that can drive someone to lose everything he's just won.

'During my day at the casino I learnt a few home truths. By and large, gambling isn't about high-rollers winning and losing vast amounts of money. Casinos survive on regular customers who win or lose £100 a night. Gamblers fall into two groups – the sane and the degenerate. The sane gambler can win £1,000 in a night, pocket half and then spread the remainder over a number of tables to minimise any future loss. He will keep most of his winnings because he sees it as his wages. If a degenerate wins £1000 he will carry on until he has lost the lot, because the winnings were never real to him. The manageress told me that she could tell when someone has come in to her casino to lose, because instead of covering bets with various permutations, he bets on single numbers. Losing is all part of the way the gambling addict confirms his self-hatred and punishes himself for it.

'One of the saddest stories I was told was of a man who had been given £50 by his wife to buy sand-shoes for the kids as they were off on holiday the next day. He went to the betting shop and lost the lot. He then borrowed £150 from a loan shark in the bookies and lost that. He had to go back home to tell his family that not only were there no sand-shoes for the kids, but he'd also had to cancel the holiday to repay the money. When I heard this, the idea of Fitz forging Judith's signature on the bank details to increase the mortgage made perfect sense, and I came to terms with that part of his character.'

Forensic psychology was not quite so easy to assimilate. Most people think they have a good idea of what psychology is, but in reality many of them would be hard pushed to tell the difference between a psychiatrist, who treats people with an illness to be treated or cured by drugs, and a psychologist, who views people's behaviour as variations of the normal and tries to get them to understand it and develop strategies to cope with it. Robbie probably knew more about psychology, and indeed forensic psychology, than most lay people, having read numerous articles on offender profiling, but he wanted to get a fixed idea of what a forensic psychologist did, and how he behaved, before filming started. 'Even though it was a TV drama, nothing would have been worse than to have given a performance that alienated every trained criminal psychologist in the country.'

The man whom Robbie approached was Ian Stephen who was then working as the Director of Psychological Services at the State Hospital in Carstairs - the Scottish equivalent of Broadmoor. Ian Stephen became a forensic psychologist almost by accident. He had studied psychology at Aberdeen University, but had become disillusioned with it, doubting that it had any real application in the outside world, and decided to teach foreign languages instead. Two years later, in the early 1960's, he felt that a use for his training had emerged, and he took a postgraduate degree in educational psychology. 'I was working in a fairly deprived and depressed area of Glasgow, and I suppose that it was inevitable that much of my time was spent with adolescents and their families who were in trouble with the law,' says Ian. 'At that time there wasn't a clear forensic identity for psychologists, and sometime in the late '60s, even though I was still employed by the Education Department, I became involved in a research project funded by the Scottish Office working in a forensic clinic.' In 1969 Ian was asked to join the forensic clinic on a full-time basis. He accepted the offer and has worked with offenders ever since.

Curiously, it was a series of events that had started in February 1968 that brought Robbie and Ian together. It was as part of Ian's work at the Forensic Psychiatry Unit that he was asked by Dr Robert Brittain, the psychiatrist in charge, to help, in a pre-computerised attempt at a profile, to find a killer nicknamed 'Bible John', who had murdered three women in the city. 'Bible John' picked up his victims at dance halls and then strangled them. His nickname was acquired because it was believed that the killer used to introduce himself as John and would then quote from the Bible. The police were having no luck with their enquiry, and asked Robert and Ian to interview suspects who were being held on remand for other charges.

'This was a clever move,' says Ian, 'because, as we now know, a great many serial killers are only caught after being picked up for unrelated offences. We spoke to a number of prisoners, but we were unable to bring 'Bible John' to justice. However, we were sure that we had interviewed him. It may have been intuition on our part, but everything about one suspect seemed to fit our profile. He was a shy, quiet married man with strong religious tendencies, who had been picked up for a comparatively minor sexual offence. The police didn't have enough evidence to pin the killings to him, and he wasn't charged. We'll never know for certain that it was him, but I don't believe it was coincidence that the killings stopped when this man was placed in a secure hospital following a separate incident.'

February 1993 marked the 25th anniversary of the killings, and the *Glasgow Evening Times* decided to run a centre page spread about offender profiling, in which Ian was prominently featured. Robbie read the article and a week later Ian got a call from him asking if he could meet for a chat. So one evening later that month Robbie and Ian sat down at the bar of a Glasgow hotel to drink Diet Coke and discuss the two subjects dear to Ian's heart - jazz and forensic psychology. Robbie asked the questions, and Ian, in what was an unfamiliar role for him, provided the answers. 'By the end of the evening I felt as if every bit of background and knowledge had been drawn out by an expert researching his work,' said Ian.

Robbie and Ian covered all the different areas of forensic psychology. Contrary to popular perception there is more to the profession than catching serial killers. After all, there just aren't enough to go round to keep every criminal psychologist in business. Offender profiling is the dazzling strand of forensic psychology and is dealt with in detail in the next chapter, but much of the day to day work is concerned with either helping offenders come to terms with their crimes and their sentences, and giving them the skills to cope without re-offending when they are released, or providing psychological assessments for court appearances.

Once the scope of the job had been defined, the way was clear for the two men to move on to how Ian did his job, which for Robbie, would be the key to how he played Fitz the psychologist. 'One of the first things Robbie asked was where I would sit when conducting an interview with a prisoner,' said Ian. 'This might seem like a small detail, but in fact it was a very intelligent question. A psychologist should always arrange the furniture in the room before a session. Ideally speaking the most non-threatening set-up is to have no barriers between you and the prisoner, but sometimes you need them. On one occasion I was saved by a table and the position of a chair. I was talking to a prisoner with a history of hostage taking whom I had seen before, when suddenly the mood in the room darkened and I knew I was in an extremely vulnerable position. The prison was in the process of being rebuilt so there were no emergency buttons to get me out, and the officer who was supposed to be keeping an eye on me had been called away elsewhere. For two and a half hours I had to use all my professionalism to conceal my anxiety and stop him taking me hostage. Eventually someone came to let me out, but undoubtedly the two saving graces were that I had known the prisoner before, and that I had arranged the room with a table between us and my chair close to the door.'

Practical details such as these are in many ways textbook psychology, but much of Ian's knowledge stems more from the accumulated experience of 25 years working with offenders than any standard guidelines. 'Obviously there are models of practice,' says Ian, 'but within them there is a tremendous scope for getting things right and wrong. The longest session I would prefer to have with anyone is an hour, and if I felt that someone was of limited intelligence and had a short attention span I would tend to break the session into periods of twenty minutes, possibly stretching them over a period of days. If you go on any longer than this you can get into the problems of "Suggestibility" that have been at the centre of cases where the only evidence is a confession. In some instances the police have interviewed a suspect for up to six hours, and if one is under pressure for that length of time many people will agree to almost anything.

'When I interview an offender for the first time I will always make a point of introducing myself and telling him who I am and why I'm talking to him. Scotland is a small place and I've been working with offenders a long time so I often find that my reputation precedes me, but nevertheless it's important to start off with a mutual understanding of why we're both there. This is especially so when I'm called upon to do pre-trial psychological tests for the Crown or the defence. I wouldn't go into the details of what I had been asked to assess, like how I thought a suspect would react to the news of his wife's sudden death, but I would always make it clear on whose behalf I was acting.

'One of the problems for a forensic psychologist is to find a dividing line between becoming immune to the horror of an offence and letting the nature of it colour the way you treat an offender. If you find yourself saying to an offender who has admitted killing someone: "Only One? Fine," and moving on without reacting to the seriousness of this, then you are on dodgy ground. It can be more difficult than it seems though, because offenders aren't the beasts and monsters that popular opinion would often have them be. The effect of calling someone a beast is to make them seem mad, bad, and different, and to set them apart from you. Yet this isn't the reality. In the same way that concentration camp guards were shown to be quite normal people who could be persuaded and driven to acts of atrocity, rather than the dangerously ill psychopaths we longed to see, so most killings will have their own sense of logic, however perverse, behind them.

'Indeed, I have known of killings that I would almost class as rational. There was one very bright woman I saw who was in fear of her husband and felt she couldn't leave him because if she did he would come after her and their children. She poisoned her husband, and nearly got away with it - the murder only being discovered when her husband's relatives insisted on an exhumation. I couldn't condone her actions, but given the constraints of her circumstances and her personality, they made perfect sense. She knew exactly what she had done and why. I never felt she would re-offend and all our work was centred on finding a way for her to come to terms with her sentence without becoming corrupted by the prison system.

'Apart from some of the more bizarre multiple murderers, most killers are fairly normal people who have been forced to face the darkest side of their personality through an inability to contain everyday emotions like anger, love, hate, and greed. Yet, even though the majority of us have never killed how can we say that there could never be any circumstances when we wouldn't do the same? One question I am commonly asked by murderers who are about to be released on to the streets is: "How do I know I won't do it again?" My reply is always: "How do I know what's going to happen to me? How do I know where my breaking point is? You've done it once. Maybe it's more likely to be me that kills."

'Helping people come to terms with what they've done and finding ways to cope in the future can be an extremely slow process. Some of my work at the moment is at Shotts, Scotland's main long-term prison for difficult offenders, and there I'm working with some offenders that I've known for 10 years or more. One of the key things is to establish a level of trust, and this can be difficult because most offenders have very little experience of this. The woman poisoner and I used to have an ongoing joke about this throughout our sessions. "When will I know you trust me?" she would ask. "When I let you make me a cup of coffee," I would reply. I often find that an offender will give me a little piece of information that he hasn't told anyone else, and use it as a test, to see if it turns up elsewhere in conversations with prison staff and other offenders. This pattern can repeat itself for a long time until that person trusts your confidentiality.

'To get the best out of offenders, you mustn't allow them to feel on the defensive. I always try to let them feel as if they are interviewing me rather than vice versa. When I get to an area they are having problems with, I may back off. If you try to force an issue, you scare them off and they will never come back to it. Some offenders find it hard to accept what they've done, so there may be a denial phase to be dealt with. Rather than trying to batter them into an acceptance of their actions, I try to discover the antecedents of the crime by looking into their background and attitudes.

'Offenders are often extremely angry, both about what they have done and what has been done to them, and the psychologist has to be able to contain it. Many is the time a prisoner has told me: "How should I know? You're the psychologist." when I've asked him how he was feeling. Ranting and raving and throwing things is by no means uncommon either, and when it happens I try to give prisoners the space to be angry and sit there and take it, because it's rarely me that they're actually angry with. Once they've calmed down, you can talk about it and that's when you make the real progress. Experience counts for a great deal with such offenders. Most officers' first instinct is to pull a prisoner out of a session and take him back to the cells when they hear a lot of shouting and swearing, and you must have their confidence that you are in control of the situation.

'Empathy is one of the most effective forms of communication with an offender. I don't pretend to know exactly how a person feels, but I try to let him know that I have an understanding of what might be going on with him. I might do it by suggesting: "Did you feel such and such at that point?" and he might say: "Yeah. How did you know?" I know because I've worked with so many different offenders that I've built up a subconscious data base of common feelings. For instance, especially in particularly weird cases of sexual assault, like strangling young boys, offenders have often told me that they felt as if there was a power circuit, almost an epileptic seizure without the fit, building up in their bodies prior to the assault. So if I was talking to such an offender, I'd say something like: "How did your body feel?" Then I'd follow up with a response which suggests there may have been that type of sensation with "Like a dynamo charging?". This could well be a way of showing empathy and guiding him to defining his emotional build-up to the offence.

'Contrary to what many professional forensic psychologists might say in public, I believe that straightforward intuition, based on years of experience, can play an important role. I often get a gut feeling when someone is telling the truth; it's not something I can necessarily substantiate or corroborate, but it can help to determine the way I deal with a prisoner from then on. I've seen people two days into a long sentence and known that they won't offend again. Likewise, protesting their innocence is often part of the denial process for prisoners when they are first convicted, but there was one in particular whom I believed. Most prisoners give up after a while, but this man is still maintaining his innocence ten years later, and I'm convinced that my initial intuition was correct.'

While Ian spoke, Robbie's tape recorder ground on relentlessly, and when the two men parted company at the end of the evening, Robbie went home to absorb the information. It was never going to be a simple question of Robbie trying to make Ian into Fitz, because Fitz's character was already largely defined before Ian and Robbie met. Indeed, Ian and Fitz could hardly be more different. Ian is a calm, quiet, 55-year-old man who has been happily married for over 25 years, only drinks whisky in moderation, and for whom 'as a true Aberdonian' parting with money is not high on his agenda. Fitz is the exact opposite, and what is worse, has, according to Gub Neal, a creator in Jimmy McGovern who was 'only happy if he was torturing him. Jimmy couldn't even let Fitz have a straightforward, no questions asked, choice of a one night stand with Penhaligon. In *One Day a Lemming Will Fly* the choice is two weeks away and a broken marriage, which is far more complicated.'

Armed with Ian's information, Robbie set out to establish Fitz's own reasons for becoming a forensic psychologist and his *modus operandi*. 'The romantic in Fitz is interested in the pure motive - the why and how, but the cynic in him just loves to be right and rub peoples' noses in it, and psychology fulfils both needs for him perfectly. He has chosen forensic psychology because he likes the excitement of crime. Finding out why someone has committed a series of murders or rapes is fundamentally more attractive to him than why someone has nicked a pair of tights or has left his wife. He was probably something of an iconoclast twenty years ago; his friends would say that he just hasn't grown up, but he would say they were dull and boring. He likes to explain himself intellectually, but in fact it is often his gut instinct that gets to the heart of a case. Unlike Ian, though, Fitz despises this intuition.'

For Robbie the goal was not to imitate real life, but to interpret it within the context of the character he was playing. This is perfectly illustrated by the immensely strong scene in *Mad Woman in the Attic* when Fitz is interviewing the amnesiac whilst Penhaligon is in the room. Fitz is trying to get him to remember by getting him to imagine Penhaligon as a potential victim. He starts a scatter gun attack on Penhaligon by hypothesising about her first sexual experience and how ashamed she felt. The power of the scene lies partly in the accuracy of Fitz's attack which clearly leaves Penhaligon deeply wounded. Ian would never use such cheap tactics. There's a fair probability that most women recall their first sexual experience with something less than unqualified pleasure, but Ian wouldn't capitalize on this to score points over a colleague and to empathise with an offender.

The psychologist Fitz that emerged may have been unusual and unlikely, but as far as Ian was concerned he was credible. 'Cracker was never intended to be a documentary, and not only does the time span of interviewing offenders get severely condensed, but Fitz also transgresses many codes of conduct and gets away with it. I can't say I've ever come across a psychologist like him, but he's a convincing amalgam of different people because I've certainly seen bits of Fitz in all sorts of psychologists. If the young Fitz were to turn up as a student for an interview for a clinical psychology course, he might have a bit of a problem getting on because of his personality. He's a man with a hint of danger whose pathological element could identify quite closely with offenders. I would hesitate to call it empathy because I'm not sure if personality disorders can be said to have empathy! The main thing is that Fitz's character is incredibly attractive to many professional psychologists, though I'm sure that they wouldn't own up to it. Most psychologists are quiet, introverted types who secretly long to say and do the things Fitz does but who are restrained by their professionalism.

'At times it would be difficult to imagine how prisoners would cope with such a strong aggressive personality as Fitz. His technique in interviewing the amnesiac in Mad Woman in the Attic was to shout and be confrontative which is very different to the one that I would adopt, but the sort of questions he asked are quite similar. Amnesia is a problem for a forensic psychologist, because it's difficult to know whether the person is deliberately choosing not to remember, or is waiting until it's past being inconvenient not to, and there's always a tendency to look on it with suspicion. I have had some genuine cases, though. One man could remember everything up till a few minutes prior to his offence and then nothing until he woke up somewhere else, and I spent a lot of time with a serial sex offender trying to remember specific events. Whether it's actual amnesia, a drugs or alcohol black-out, or a psychological blockage caused by events being too horrific and painful to remember, is hard to tell.

'My first reaction to someone claiming amnesia would be to test his immediate memory skills by asking questions like "Who is the Prime Minister?" to determine his level of function. I would then spend time winning his trust by asking all sorts of questions about everything other than the offence. I would ask him about his family and childhood, what he thought he was doing in prison, what sort of music he liked. I would be trying to get him in the habit of communicating with me about things that weren't threatening. Once his guard was down and he was feeling relaxed, I would try throwing in some more pointed questions like "What were you doing on Saturday night?" to see how he reacted. To make this seem as casual as possible I would probably be looking out of the window when I said it. If he responded positively I would pursue it, but if he got angry and suspicious I would back off and move on to something innocuous again.

'The questioning would continue like this over a long series of interviews, and eventually, either the suspect would begin to remember, or I would become convinced one way or the other about the authenticity of the amnesia. If it was the latter, it would be based very much on a gut instinct because as I've said, I can get a feel for whether someone is being genuine.'

In *Mad Woman in the Attic* it is this same intuition as much as his belief that a priest would not break the confessional that convinces Fitz that the amnesia is genuine and that the monk is innocent even before the last interview takes place. When the monk finally remembers what happened on the train and can say: "I didn't do it", Fitz replies: "I know that."

Ian never told Robbie what to do, but he believes his influences can be clearly detected within Robbie's acting. 'The way in which Robbie incorporated what he had been able to extract from our discussions into his own forensic psychologist role within Fitz's personality without the joins being evident was remarkable. There was one scene in *To Say I Love You* where Fitz is called in from the next door cell, where he was cooling off after his arrest, to help deal with Sean who had been brought in for hi-jacking a bus. Sean had been interviewed by DS Beck who had harassed him and made him confused and hysterical. Fitz manages to gain his trust and confidence and calm him down. He let Sean come to him and need him. It was a brilliant piece of acting, but I would be very surprised if Robbie had worked it all out for himself. If he had, he should have been a psychologist rather than an actor.'

In his interviews with Tina in *To Say I Love You* and Cassidy in *One Day a Lemming Will Fly*, Fitz shows that he understands how they both feel by talking about the crimes in terms he thinks have meaning for them. The idea is that once they know he can empathise, he can then challenge them. Ian is full of admiration for the way that Robbie handled this too, though he admits that his challenges are more aggressive than he himself would make. 'Even if I knew an offender well, the furthest I would go by way of confrontation is to say: "Who do you think you're trying to kid?".'

The difference between Fitz's handling of the interviews with Tina and Cassidy, of course, is that Cassidy is innocent. This, too, Ian finds believable. 'As much as we all try to avoid becoming so convinced that we can't see beyond our own noses, we can all sometimes set up our hypotheses so that we can't change them. When you do this you can lose sight of the obvious; police assessments are often like this, and we can do the same. The real world is full of imponderables, and psychologists are not infallible.'

Ian has never worked with the police in the way that Fitz does. His associations with them have been far more informal, with certain officers phoning him with questions, or popping round to his office for a quiet chat about a particular case. However, his experiences of police attitudes towards his work mirror those in *Cracker*. 'You get the Bilborough type, the young intellectual who can recognise the value of psychology and probably likes to think he's a bit of a psychologist himself. He won't necessarily like you because you represent a bit of a challenge to his authority, but he will listen to what you've got to say. Then you get the DS Beck type who thinks that all psychologists are a waste of time, and that good old-fashioned police work, together with some heavy questioning in the cells, will solve the problem.'

The tension in the relationship between the psychologist and the police is superbly portrayed in the clash of personalities between Fitz and Bilborough after DS Giggs has been found murdered in *To Say I Love You*. Bilborough knows that he needs Fitz's help, but he hates him for it, and when it is Fitz who is asked to appear on the *Lenny Lyon Show*, the local chat show, Bilborough can scarcely contain his envy and anger that it wasn't him that was asked. Whether a psychologist would deliberately disobey police orders and release a profile on TV when he had been specifically asked to wait until the next day before doing so, as Fitz does on the *Lenny Lyon Show*, is highly questionable, but forensic psychologists are certainly beginning to get a much more prominent media presence.

This is something that gives Ian some cause for concern. 'The media likes to deal in definites, and psychology cannot do that. Only recently I saw Paul Britton, an immensely respected forensic psychologist, appear on *Crimewatch* making a direct TV appeal to a rapist by saying: "I know that you're out there and that you want to talk to me". It was almost like something out of an American movie. I could see the point of what he was trying to do, but it felt more like a piece of media dramatic effect than a clinical way of going about things.'

Ian had no idea after he parted company with Robbie that he would have any further involvement with *Cracker*, and was surprised to get a phone call four months later asking for more help. What he did, and the way that he reconciled it with his professional standing, are documented in an article he wrote called *Robbie, Fitz, and Me - A Venture into Television*, published in the January 1994 issue of *The Psychologist*. Here he takes up the story after his first meeting with Robbie.

'"That's that", I thought. It had been very enjoyable meeting and interesting talking with Robbie, but I did not expect much else to follow.

Then at the end of June a high profile London-based press and public relations firm phoned on behalf of Granada Television, inviting me to the studios and on location in Manchester to meet with the production team and discuss further involvement with *Cracker*, and in particular with the publicity for the programme. This set off a few panic buttons in me in terms of what I was letting myself in for. I think a lot of psychologists, including myself, have misgivings about involvement with the media because of the way the profession might be so easily misrepresented when others are reinterpreting for lay consumers what they have divulged in good faith. I also had concerns about personal exposure and the knock-on effects of that. However, despite my first inclination to back off, I agreed to the visit.

'There I had the opportunity to talk to the producer, Gub Neal, other members of the production team, Robbie again, and the PR firm. I found them genuinely interested in the issues for the profession and in the way psychologists work, and I took the opportunity to do some education. In turn I was educated on production and PR needs. I read the scripts, saw some of the location work and found any comments I made were positively listened to. Overall I was impressed by the desire to produce a quality programme and became confident in the responsible manner in which they wished to use me further in a consultancy role. I therefore agreed to take up their invitation. I did, however, speak to Mary McMurran, Secretary of the Division of Criminological and Legal Psychology, to advise her of what was happening and to get some professional reassurance for continuing with the exercise.

'The next phase of the operation was the contact with the press for the building up to the programme. The PR company defined who I could talk to in this period, and this culminated with the press launch on September 1 where the first story of two episodes was shown to a large group representing all the main newspapers, followed by all the principal people involved, including myself, being available for interview by the journalists. They again reduced my trepidation further by avoiding the sensationalist approach and concentrating on the professional background and the reality of the relationship between the fictional character and myself.'

*   *   *   *

'Both here and in subsequent contacts with the press, interviews focused on the learning relationship between Robbie Coltrane and myself, and the contrasts between my own lifestyle and professional approach and that portrayed in the drama. The other thing I had to come to terms with in the course of my involvement was that the series did not claim to be a documentary. In addition my concerns about verisimilitude had to be set aside (but hopefully not too far) for dramatic effect within the confines of the story length - as opposed to it being a day in the life of yours truly. This, although interesting enough, would have had viewers in search of entertainment rapidly changing channels. After all, I rationalised, police, doctors, lawyers have all had high profile series with poetic licence being used, so why not psychologists?

'All these issues were raised in interview, as indeed were professional codes of practice, the real work of forensic psychology, and its emergence as a speciality within Registration and possible developing roles for practitioners. What also impressed me watching Robbie Coltrane in action with the press was the way he could describe the role of a psychologist accurately - obviously derived from his background research - and he seemed to be doing a very effective PR job for the profession. The production team made it clear they valued the credibility for the programme that would be gained by my professional contribution and the media certainly paid heed to this. My initial concerns decreased as my own confidence in channelling the flow of interviews increased. I recognised the themes regularly arising and became more rehearsed in providing answers which avoided my being led into naive overstatements by enthusiastic story seekers.

'It became clear after this promotion that the series was going to make a significant impact. Initial anxieties that the programme might not catch on were allayed and it was really satisfying to see viewing figures over the first few weeks move to over 12 million. The response of the public seems to have been quite positive and personally I have been encouraged by non-professionals talking to me about the programme and also showing me that the PR about forensic psychology in its broadest sense has made some educational impact. As the series' success has become apparent, so has the interest by the press in the background to the character, Fitz, and in the general theme of forensic psychology. Although trying to maintain a professional objectivity by concentrating on issues and themes in the interviews, I have had to come to terms with the personalisation that emerges in the completed articles.

'The response from professional colleagues has generally been one of quiet amusement, but they have been interested and supportive with it. I do get the feeling, however, that the majority would prefer to avoid the risk of public exposure themselves, and become anxious when they see others doing it for fear of possible diminution of the profession's standing. I must admit I share some of these concerns myself, but have grown to recognise, in the course of my involvement with *Cracker*, that there are benefits to be had by the profession in learning the skills of communicating through the media to the lay public in addition to our normal academic and scientific presentation modes.

'I found it an interesting and positive experience - I was probably lucky in being involved in a top-class programme - which would certainly reduce my fears for any subsequent involvement. One must, however, keep things in perspective and not get too carried away with the hype and transitory attention - although I must admit the mention I got from Robbie on the Steve Wright show on Radio One raised me in status with my offsprings' friends. With these reservations I would say to colleagues it is worth taking a risk from time to time. Have a go, it can be fun.'

If Ian still had any doubts about his involvement with *Cracker* when he wrote this article, they ended with its publication. 'To be given space in such a respected professional journal as *The Psychologist* was a good indication that I hadn't compromised my ethics and that I was still respected by my colleagues,' said Ian, 'and when I was asked to help on the second series I had no hesitation in accepting.' Even though his role has now grown from just advising Robbie to commenting on possible story-lines and discussing the likely behaviour patterns of other central characters like DS Penhaligon and DS Beck, Ian remains modest about his contribution. 'I'm delighted to have been able to help, but don't forget that *Cracker* is a TV drama. Any success it has had is principally down to the writer, actors, and producers, not to me.' This may be so, but everyone on *Cracker* breathed a huge sigh of relief when Ian Stephen decided to become involved.

CHAPTER 4
OFFENDER PROFILING

WHENEVER A PARTICULARLY brutal murder is committed, one of the first questions the investigating officer is often asked is: 'Do you have a profile for the suspect?' Offender profiling captured the imagination of the press and public in the late 1980s, but unlike many new ideas that are fashionable for a while and then forgotten, this one is here to stay. The reason for this is that offender profiling works.

People who commit certain types of crime tend to have childhood backgrounds and patterns of behaviour in common, and if these characteristics are properly understood by detectives, they can be used either to eliminate possible suspects from an enquiry or to focus police attention on to certain individuals. In May 1994 Robert Black was convicted of the murders of Susan Maxwell, Caroline Hogg, and Sarah Harper, and he is still under suspicion for up to ten further murders, including that of Genette Tate who vanished while on her newspaper round in 1978. It was a stroke of luck that led to his arrest. An observant eye-witness, David Herkes, caught him in the act of abducting a six-year-old girl in a Scottish border town in 1990, and phoned the police. No proper profile was ever drawn up for these murders, partly because it wasn't common practice at the time. Had there been a profile, though, the chances are that it would have fitted Black like a glove as he was almost the identikit child murderer, and his arrest might not have owed anything to chance.

There would have been no prizes for guessing that Black was likely to be a lone male who had problems relating to women, and indeed he was. He rented an attic room in Stamford Hill, London, in which he kept child pornography, rarely had visitors, and had no sense of personal hygiene. Yet there would have been other more telling clues about him. Child-killers generally build up to murder by committing less serious sex crimes earlier in their criminal careers. At 16 Black received a conviction for 'lewd and libidinous' behaviour towards a young girl, and four years later he was jailed for an indecent assault on the six-year-old daughter of his landlord. Likewise, the large distances between crime scenes would have indicated something about the murderer. Far from suggesting a maniac who roamed the country at random, the distances pointed to someone who had good reason to travel - like a travelling salesman or lorry driver. Robert Black had been employed as a staff van driver for two companies, before becoming a freelance driver.

One of the problems with profiles as far as the lay public is concerned is that not only can they seem incredibly obvious with hindsight, which is when most cases have come to the public's attention, but they are often presented in an extremely simplistic format. Yet profiling can be highly sophisticated. Once you had seen the video camera evidence, you wouldn't have needed to be Sigmund Freud or Melanie Klein to have worked out that the killers of two-year-old toddler Jamie Bulger were between 10-12 years old, came from problem

Bilborough, Fitz, Penhaligon and Beck. The characters developed along with the story lines.

'He chases women, but as soon as he's caught one, he's bored again' was how writer Jimmy McGovern described Fitz.

Bilborough was seen as a good cop, but he still knowingly sent the wrong man to prison.

When Fitz accused Beck of having a moustache to disguise his homosexual tendencies, it nearly got Jimmy McGovern beaten up.

A Mad Woman in the Attic. Fitz travelled with the amnesiac murder victim to visit a woman who claimed to be his wife.

To Say I Love You. Fitz brings his psychological weight to bear during an interview.

Fitz - icon of a new religion?

Fitz discusses starting prices with his mum.

By some standards, Fitz is almost a conventional family man.

Fitz falls foul of Penhaligon, having finally pushed her too far.

Fitz cheats death in To Say I Love You.

More effective use of his experience as a psychologist might have helped
Fitz avoid a beating in a gambling den.

Robbie Coltrane with forensic psychologist Ian Stephen.

Fitz refines his interview technique.

families and liked to bunk off school. But Dr Paul Britton, one of Britain's leading forensic psychologists, was able to tell the police immediately after Jamie went missing that 'in due course they (one of the two boys) will want to say that the other child was the active agent while they were passive or opposed to the assaults.' He was also able to provide the following list of insights into why the two boys committed the crime, all of which turned out to be accurate.

1. They formed a club of two, talked it through with each other in general terms: 'Why don't we?...', 'I bet we could....', 'Wouldn't it be good if?...'.

2. Their excitement at being able to control the child would have been sufficiently rewarding to outweigh any feelings of compassion or response to knowledge of wrong-doing - they enjoyed it too much to stop.

3. It has certain similarities with those circumstances where children set out, often in group, to find, torture, and finally kill frogs and cats. It is intended and enjoyed, and the victims are reduced to unimportant opportunities for pleasure.

4. After the killing and the arrangement of the body, the arousal will have dissipated, giving way to feelings of anxiety, fearfulness, and sometimes exhilaration.

5. Not primarily any sexual motivation - the issues were control, excitement, and sadism.

None of this information was immediately obvious to the police, but it was useful in pinpointing the type of boys they were looking for, and vital for interviewing them once they had been found. Dr Britton's predictions might seem too good to be true to an outsider, but they owe nothing to luck and everything to a sound understanding of both juveniles and the criminal mind. Ian Stephen, the forensic psychologist who advised on *Cracker*, explains how Paul Britton would have reached his conclusions.

'It's extremely common for one child to blame the other once they have been caught doing something wrong and are under pressure, so Dr Britton would have felt on safe ground with this. It's almost an automatic, straightforward behavioural response to try to distance yourself from the crime and pass the responsibility on to someone else. I would also expect the one who cried "It wasn't me" the loudest to be the leader of the two boys, because he would be the most skilled at passing the blame.

'Forming a club is a normal way in which young boys relate to each other, so again this would not be difficult to predict. Most kids like to operate as a peer group, be it the scouts, guides, or gangs. The more unclubbable or anti-social kids who aren't accepted into larger groups tend to form their own sub-groups with their own sets of rules.

'By saying the two boys enjoyed it too much to stop, Dr Britton means that the initial buzz that all kids get from doing something a bit naughty gathered a momentum of its own and developed into a compulsion which was almost impossible to stop. This is common in all attacks of this type.

'The comparison with killing frogs and cats reflects what we know about serial killers, as many have enjoyed hurting animals at some time in their lives. They tend to see animals as objects rather than living things, and enjoy the feelings of power over something helpless. Indeed I would be surprised if the two boys had not tortured animals at some time before their abduction of Jamie Bulger, because it would be unusual for an attack of that ferocity to have been committed without some form of prior experience of this sort.

'The last two points are also textbook forensic psychology. The dissipation of excitement is something that is often experienced by people who kill strangers, and while I'm not too sure about the sexual nature of Jamie Bulger's murder, all killings have some sexual content. Heterosexual men tend to kill women, gay men kill men, and bisexuals are indiscriminate. So with the Bulger case there would have been some sexual motivation, though most likely on a subconscious level, as the two boys were of an age when they would not have been that sexually self-aware.'

Given that such detailed and skilful analyses are on offer, two questions come to mind. Why weren't they used by the police sooner than the mid-1980s, and how are they compiled? Or to put it another way, why, in the 1970s, weren't we all watching programmes like *Cracker* that explore the darker side of human motivation instead of those like *The Sweeney* where cops achieve their results through an excess of adrenalin and violence? The truth is that just as TV programmes tend to reflect current trends, so different strands of psychology are at the mercy of fashion, and for a long time forensic psychology was deeply unhip.

Just because a subject is unfashionable, though, it doesn't mean that no one is thinking about it, and there were some early noteworthy attempts to define the likely characteristics of some notorious criminals. In Donald Rumbelow's book, *The Complete Jack the Ripper*, he chronicles a letter sent from a Dr Thomas Bond in 1888 to Robert Anderson, the head of the London CID, which speculates on the sort of man 'Jack the Ripper' might be.

'He must in my opinion be a man subject to periodic

attacks of homicidal and erotic mania. The character of the mutilations indicate that the man may be in a condition sexually, that may be called Satyriasis. It is of course possible that the homicidal impulse may have developed from a revengeful or brooding condition of the mind, or that religious mania may have been the original disease but I do not think that either hypothesis is likely. The murderer in external appearance is quite likely to be a quiet inoffensive looking man probably middle-aged and neatly and respectably dressed. I think he might be in the habit of wearing a cloak or overcoat or he could hardly have escaped notice in the streets if the blood on his hands or clothes were visible.

'Assuming the murderer to be such a person as I have just described, he would be solitary and eccentric in his habits; also he is likely to be a man without regular occupation, but with some small income or pension. He is possibly living among respectable persons who have some knowledge of his character and habits and who may have grounds for suspicion that he is not quite right in his mind at times.'

History does not relate how seriously Dr Bond's profile was taken by the police, nor, since the identity of 'Jack the Ripper' is still in dispute, how accurate. However, what we do know is that the FBI produced a remarkably similar profile one hundred years later. One profile that was uncannily accurate was that of the 'Mad Bomber of New York' who terrorised the city for over ten years in the 1950s. Dr Brussel, an American psychiatrist, predicted that the culprit would be an East European immigrant in his forties who lived with his mother in Connecticut. He would adore his mother and hate his father, be extremely neat and tidy, and would wear a double-breasted suit. When George Metesky was finally caught, he was indeed wearing a double-breasted suit, and fitted the profile in many other ways besides.

Despite the occasional success, as far as the police were concerned profiling remained on a par with weirdos phoning up to say that the wanted person was an Aries, or something equally obscure. Thanks, but no thanks. That profiling was viewed this way says a lot about the entrenched views the police had of their work, but also a lot about profiling itself at the time. Even though a profile may have been accurate, it was generally built on insight and intuition rather than hard evidence or scientific data, and there was little sense that even psychologists regarded them as being that reliable.

Prior to the 1970s, forensic psychology had always been regarded as something of a backwater within the profession, and as a consequence there was little interest in, or under-standing of, criminal behaviour. This disinterest reached its apotheosis with the work of the American psychologist, Abraham Maslow, in the 1960s. He proposed that psycho-logical theory had by and large been determined by the study of the neurotic or the 'psychologically unwell', and that if you wanted to find out what potential humans have, you should look at those people who have achieved. To this end he made case studies of famous men and women, both dead and alive, and from these concluded a five tier hierarchy of human needs. Maslow's work was full of value judgements. It made assumptions about what is sick and what is well, and by studying the famous he equated achievement with fulfilled potential. Is a public figure with a disastrous private life a ful-filled person? Despite these very obvious flaws, Maslow's work captured the spirit of his age, and forensic psychology continued to take a back seat.

The few criminal psychologists who were practising at this time were constrained in what they could do by their enthusiasm for the Skinnerian behavioural conditioning model that dominated psychological thinking. It was felt that psychologists could only treat the behaviour they observed, and that by punishing bad behaviour and rewarding the good, criminals could be reformed. Consequently, psychologists began to suggest all sorts of treatments, like aversion therapy, that blatantly infringed civil liberties. The most famous example of this in Britain was in the 1960s in Wakefield maximum security prison, where prisoners started off with nothing, and had to earn the right to everything from clothes to a bed.

Such practices may seem absurdly dated now, but few people seriously challenged them at the time because behaviourism was the accepted prevailing trend in psychology. Indeed forensic psychology was still in its infancy, struggling to find a theoretical framework for itself, and such a rigid adherence to current fashion was more than understandable in the circumstances. The breakthrough for forensic psychology came in the early '70s when practitioners came to have the confidence to adopt a more flexible approach to their work. Instead of just looking at the behaviour they could see, psychologists realized that they could also work with the thoughts and ideas behind a person's actions without going into the realms of psychoanalysis, and that by combining the two approaches they had something of real value to offer. Offenders could now be helped to understand what their problem was and to develop ways of coping, and the prison system began to reflect this. Out went the harsh isolation regimes that had proved singularly ineffective at rehabilitation, and in came special units like that at Barlinnie in

Scotland, which Ian Stephen helped to develop, and was made famous in Jimmy Boyle's book *A Sense of Freedom*.

One of the by-products that came from helping prisoners to understand their behaviour, was that the forensic psychologists themselves developed a far greater insight into both the thoughts and actions of criminals, from their childhood up until the offence for which they had been arrested. The more offenders they interviewed the more psychologists could determine certain consistent patterns of thought and behaviour linking similar crimes, and it was this knowledge that formed the basis of a more scientific approach to offender profiling.

The traditional approach to crime dictated that the only clues of any value to be found at the scene was hard, tangible evidence like bloodstains, saliva, semen, textile fibres, finger prints, and footprints. At the core of offender profiling is the notion that each crime scene leaves invisible clues that point towards the suspect. Everything at a crime scene will say something about the perpetrator. The choice of victim, the location, the ferocity of the assault, what is left behind, what isn't left behind, and if the victim is still alive. What is and isn't said are all clues pointing towards a suspect, if only one knows how to read them. The task for the psychologist is to interpret these clues correctly, and to draw up a likely profile of the person who committed the crime based on his knowledge of criminal behaviour. The profile will not be able to predict that an offender will be living at 17, Acacia Avenue and be wearing Marks & Spencer boxer shorts, because only hard detective work can establish that kind of detail, but it can focus the police investigation on to the more likely suspects.

Probably the greatest example in recent British criminal history of a police investigation that paid the price both financially, and possibly in terms of human life, for ignoring the help that offender profiling could offer was the 'Yorkshire Ripper' enquiry. Robert Ressler and John Douglas, two of America's leading profile experts, were over in Britain during 1979 to talk to the British police about their work. At the time there was still enormous scepticism amongst the police about the value of psychological profiles drawn up from scene of crime photographs, and Ressler and Douglas were treated with a great deal of suspicion.

The two Americans' visit happened to coincide with the middle of the 'Ripper' enquiry. Eleven women had been attacked, eight of whom had been murdered, and the closest description the police had of the suspect was a man aged between twenty and fifty-five. One of the policemen who happened to be at Bramshill to hear the lectures was John Domaille, an investigating officer on the 'Ripper' investigation. Domaille described the crimes, and challenged Ressler and Douglas to compile an instant profile of the offender.

Ressler resisted the temptation at first because he felt that any profile he drew up without seeing the actual photos was liable to be highly suspect. However, when another policeman produced the tape recording of the man the police thought they were looking for, Ressler decided to have a go. The tape, together with two letters, had been sent directly to George Oldfield, the officer in charge of the investigation, and was taken so seriously that the tape was played on national TV. There was even a telephone number the public could ring to listen to the tape and offer any comments they had about the identity of the voice. The message on the tape ran as follows:-

'I'm Jack. I see you are still having no luck catching me. I have the greatest respect for you, George, but you are no nearer catching me now than four years ago when I started. I reckon your boys are letting you down, George; ya can't be much good, can ya? The only time they came near touching me was a few months back in Chapeltown, when I was disturbed - even if it was a uniformed copper and not a detective. I warned you in March that I'd strike again, but I couldn't get there. I'm not quite sure when I'll strike again, but it will definitely be some time this year - maybe September, October or earlier if I get the chance. There's plenty of them knocking about. They never learn, do they, George? I'll keep on going for quite a while yet. I can't see myself being nicked just yet. Even if you do get near, I'll probably top myself first. Well, it's been nice chatting to you, George.'

As the tape wound to a close Ressler turned to the assembled company and said: 'You realize, of course, that the man on the tape is not the killer, don't you?' The British police realized nothing of the sort, and in fact, ever since the tape first appeared, potential suspects were eliminated if they did not have a matching Geordie accent to the voice on the tape. Ressler then gave his reasoning for why it was a hoax. What the man on the tape said was inconsistent with the crimes. Knocking his victims unconscious and then mutilating them after death was the act of a woman hating introvert, and such a man would never get in touch with the police in this way.

Following these revelations the British policemen gathered in the pub pressed Ressler for more information about the likely killer, and though it went against his professionalism to do so without at least a photograph to go on, he was finally persuaded. Ressler predicted that the 'Ripper' would be a man in his late twenties or early thirties who had either dropped out of school or had no higher education. He had been able to get in and out of the murder areas without drawing attention or suspicion to himself because his work took him there. Therefore he was either a cabdriver, a lorry driver, a postman, or possibly even a policeman. He would not be a total loner and would have a relationship with a woman.

After Ressler had defended these conclusions, Domaille asked the two Americans to go to Yorkshire to view the scene of crime photos. They were due back in America and so were unable to do so, but offered to help out if the photos were sent back to them at the FBI headquarters in Quantico. The photos never made the transatlantic crossing, because George Oldfield was convinced that Ressler and Douglas had nothing to offer the police. The enquiry laboured on for well over another year, until Peter Sutcliffe was fortuitously apprehended. As Ressler predicted, Sutcliffe was a thirty-five year old married lorry driver who regularly travelled around the north of England in the course of his job. The hoaxer was later revealed to be a retired policeman who hated George Oldfield.

*   *   *   *

It is hard to determine exactly when offender profiling first became scientific - indeed there are those who would argue that it still isn't. Dr Robert Brittain and Ian Stephen's efforts to profile "Bible John' were probably one of the first serious attempts, since Dr Brittain had spent a great deal of time working with the more sadistic sexual offenders and as such was well placed to identify him. Indeed, as a result of this work Dr Brittain wrote one of the first ever papers on profiling called *The Sadistic Murderer* which was published in the journal *Criminal Justice and the Law* in 1970.

However, there is no doubt that the name most associated with profiling in its early days in the 1970s is Robert Ressler, who was responsible for the growth of the Behavioural Sciences Unit at the FBI headquarters in Quantico, later made famous by *Silence of the Lambs*. Indeed it was Ressler himself who coined the words 'serial killers' for those murderers who have killed three or more times with a cooling off period between each incident. Before then, such killers were known as 'stranger killers', regardless of whether the offender knew his victim or not.

Ressler had joined the army straight after leaving school, had then moved into the military police, and at the age of 35 had joined the FBI in 1970. He soon became a teacher at Quantico, lecturing in everything from abnormal psychology to hostage negotiation, and having picked up some of the ideas behind profiling, he became the FBI's chief profiler. Up till then the FBI had only paid lip service to criminal psychology; some crimes, like those for gain or of passion, were deemed to have a fairly obvious motive and so little understanding was required, while serial killers were considered to be just psychopaths. Ressler realized that a far greater understanding of the mind of the serial killer than this was necessary to convert profiling into a science.

Ressler began reading all the available material on serial killers and came to the conclusion that everything had been written either from a legal perspective or by someone who was incapable of relating psychological insight to forensic study. He spent time talking to psychiatrists and social workers who had worked with violent offenders, and once armed with sufficient background he decided to speak to the offenders themselves. 'We wanted to learn more about what factors in the killer's environment, childhood, and background made him want to commit such crimes,' wrote Ressler in his book *Whoever Fights Monsters*. 'We also wanted to know many more details about the crimes themselves - what happened during the assault, what went on immediately after the killer was certain that the victim had died, how he had chosen the site for disposal of the body. If we got enough information from enough interviewees, we'd be able to compile useful lists: so many took souvenirs, so many read or viewed pornographic materials. Then, too, there were some old chestnuts in regard to murder that we wanted to test; for instance, whether killers really did return to the scenes of their crimes.'

Ressler began his 'Criminal Personality Research Project' in 1978, and over the next few years came to interview over one hundred of America's most infamous offenders, including Sirhan Sirhan - Bobby Kennedy's assassin, Charles Manson, William Heirens - the Boston Strangler, David Berkowitz - 'Son of Sam', Edmund Kemper, Ted Bundy, and John Gacy, who was executed in early 1994 after over a decade on death row. Not every murderer was desperately forthcoming, but from time to time Ressler would learn something that gave a penetrating insight into the mind of the serial killer. David Berkowitz, the 'Son of Sam' killer, who had murdered six people in New York over the space of a year provided one such piece of information.

At Berkowitz's trial it had been generally assumed that the timings of the killings were in some way significant, but Ressler discovered that Berkowitz was actually out stalking victims on a nightly basis, but would only attack if he felt the circumstances were ideal. When he couldn't find a victim he would return to scenes of his former crimes to relive the experience. Just as Berkowitz became sexually aroused in the act of killing his victims, so too did he become excited at seeing the odd bloodstain and other trace marks of previous crimes, and would sit in his car and masturbate. This was a stunning insight for Ressler: not only did it confirm that killers did indeed return to the scene of the crime, which indicated that police observation of any crime scene could be extremely worthwhile, but it showed that the return was driven by the sexual content of the killing, rather than by guilt as had previously been assumed.

This sexual element of murder was well illustrated in the first two *Cracker* stories. In *Mad Woman in the Attic* the killer shaves the pubic hair of his victim after she has died. The sexual nature of death is even more graphic in *To Say I Love You*. After Sean has battered the loan shark to death in the alley, he and Tina have frenzied sex standing against the wall beside the body. Fitz understands this perfectly. 'Do you remember those soldiers coming back from the Falklands with all those women lining the quay waving their bras and knickers in the air? Patriotism? No - lust. Some of those men had killed and those women wanted them. What is death, Panhandle?' 'The finest aphrodisiac in the world, Dr Fitzgerald,' replies Penhaligon. There is a similar sexual content to their second killing, the murder of DS Giggs. Giggs is lured to Tina's flat by the promise of a bit on the side, only to be killed by Sean. However there is an ambivalence in Tina's actions. Her advances to Giggs are partly to eliminate a copper who was getting too close, but also, one suspects, genuinely felt because her sexual fantasies have become so entwined with killing.

David Berkowitz's revelation about returning to the scene of his crimes made a further impact on Ressler. 'I had long argued that the aberrant behaviour of killers is in some ways only an extension of normal behaviour,' he wrote. 'Every parent of an adolescent girl has observed that teenage boys will repeatedly walk or ride their bikes or drive their cars by a girl's house, or hang around as close to her as they are allowed, and engage in impetuous, spontaneous behaviour. Hanging around the scene of the crime, then, is an instance of arrested, inadequate personality development, an extension of something normal into abnormal behaviour.'

The more killers to whom Ressler spoke, the more he realized that they weren't just extraordinary monsters, however monstrous their crimes, because they all fitted into recognisable patterns that were clear variations of the norm. Loosely speaking, Ressler's findings can be summed up in an article Ian Stephen wrote entitled *What Makes Serial Killers Tick*. 'Most serial killers are young, white, and male, committing their first murder between the ages of 25 and 30. The majority usually come from broken homes with weak or absent fathers and dominant females present. They have often been deprived and/or abused physically or sexually in childhood. They have poor self-esteem - often rooted in their childhood trauma with a subsequent reactive violent fantasy. They may even enact violent fantasies in their minds including acts of murder at seven or eight years of age. They may be cruel to animals prior to turning to humans and may set fire to things.

'Many are intelligent but are underachievers with a lot of resentment and they blame others for their failure to achieve.

They long to be important. There is a suggestion that there may be some neurological abnormalities which may be the result of head injury, and enuresis may be present in child-hood. Usually there is a sexual motivation with the individual's own libido being mirrored by his victim i.e. a heterosexual killer will choose a female and a homosexual will target gays. The majority are failures with women.'

Profiling is the science of making logical deductions and inferences about any given crime, and the scene of crime remains the primary source of information for the psychologist as much as the police. That is why Ressler was so reluctant to make any predictions about the 'Yorkshire Ripper' without seeing any scene of crime photos, and why Fitz is so keen to examine the alley where the loanshark was killed for himself. Most psychologists would prefer to visit a crime scene in person rather than simply see photos - the difference between the two being like going to a football match where you get a broad, panoramic view and a sense of atmosphere or watching it on TV where you get a limited field of vision - but more often than not they have to make do with photos.

For obvious reasons photos were all Ressler had to go on in his interviews with convicted serial killers, but he was still able to formulate one central theory about killers that remains at the heart of our understanding of them, and has had a profound effect on the way profiles are constructed. All scenes of violent crime are horrific and many policeman are so overwhelmed by what they see that they are incapable of making any judgements about the killer other than: 'He must have been a psychopath.' Ressler was able to put his emotions on hold as he looked at scene after scene of death and mutilation, and began to realize that what the pictures showed were two types of serial killer: the disorganised and the organised.

Ressler recognised that some crime scenes showed signs of advance planning, which indicated an organised killer, while others had a random quality that indicated a disorganised killer. Typically, an organised killer will bring his own weapon to a crime scene, will choose his victim with some care - generally someone who approximates in size, shape, and colour to the person he has fantasized about killing, will make sure that there is a minimal risk of getting caught, will take his time over the killing, will not leave fingerprints or anything that may identify him, and will either try to conceal the body or remove it from the scene. The disorganised killer will be less selective about his victim - sometimes even choosing someone who is capable of fighting back, will come unprepared to kill and use whatever weapon comes to mind, and will often leave the body where it can be easily found.

Of course these distinctions are gross generalisations, and not every killer falls easily into either category, but they provide a useful focus for starting an investigation. The organised and disorganised killer represents very different personality types, as Ian Stephen points out: 'The organised killer is more outgoing and can form superficial relationships quite easily and might even be well thought of within the local community. He is adept at concealing his true feelings of hatred towards society and women in particular, and when he does begin a career of violence it is likely to be a stress-driven response to a particular incident. The disorganised killer conforms far more readily to the public's perception of a psychopath - indeed he may well have a history of mental illness. He will be far more of a loner due to his poor communication skills, and his personal appearance may be unkempt. His violence will be driven by internalised feelings of anger and hurt, rather than external events, and as such, the motive will be much harder to detect.'

Once the difference between personality types was grasped by Ressler, it became much easier to predict what other attributes the perpetrator of a particular crime might have. For instance, a disorganised killer is far more likely to operate locally and would tend to travel to the scene of his crime either on foot or by public transport, because he would be unlikely to have the social skills to entice anyone into his car and control them into staying whilst he drove. If, by chance, he did have a car it would probably be a mirror of his disorganised state and would be old and somewhat beaten up. Unlike the disorganised killer who will find it hard to fit into any social milieu and thus will probably be either unemployed or have a succession of low-paid menial jobs, the organised killer will have adequate social skills to hold down a minor clerical job, but insufficient skills to secure promotion. Similarly, unlike the disorganised killer who may well have no criminal record before embarking on his crimes, the organised killer will build up to his crimes gradually, and will tend to have previous convictions. The essence of the organised killer is control. He has a fantasy about the type of crime he is going to commit, and actively seeks out victims and situations where he can enact it. As each fantasy becomes reality, so he creates a new, more elaborate fantasy. So he might start by exposing himself; once he has done this he may feel emboldened enough to sexually assault someone; thereafter it might be rape; thereafter rape with torture; thereafter death. However, the organised killer's fantasies do not end with death, because each killing has to have an extra quality to the last. He learns how to get more pleasure and control from each victim, and the more accomplished he becomes the more practised he becomes at hiding his identity from the police. Each development of an obsessional fantasy takes the killer further away from the feelings that originated the fantasy, as the fantasy becomes an end in itself. From this Ressler realized that it was the earliest, rather than the most recent, murders that would tell the police the most about an organized killer. Indeed it was this piece of knowledge around which the plot for *The Silence of the Lambs* was based, for the killer's first victim is someone known to him from his home town, whereas the links between the later victims and the killer are far less obvious.

So what do the terms 'organised' and 'disorganised' tell us about the killers in *Cracker*? In *Mad Woman in the Attic* the killer shows every sign of being disorganised. The attack takes place on a crowded train where there is a good chance of getting caught, and indeed the monk interrupts the killer just before he first tries to strike. Nevertheless, once the monk has left the scene, he continues with his attack. The killing is swift and violent; disorganised killers do not like to make any emotional contact with their victims, but try to depersonalize them as quickly as possible. He then shaves the victim's pubic hair after death. This again is typical: organised killers take trophies like wallets and jewellry, whereas the disorganised tend to take souvenirs like hair or clothing, that have no discernible value.

All this puts a new slant on the way one views Fitz's interrogation of the amnesiac. The police might have thought that the amnesiac might be trying to distance himself from the killing, but Fitz would have known that the type of man who committed the murder would not have been capable of feigning amnesia. The only possibility that he was the killer was if he actually had amnesia. Hence, when Fitz realizes that the amnesia is genuine, the questioning becomes more important.

Sean and Tina, in *To Say I Love You* fit quite nicely into the organised category. It is a row with Tina's parents that precipitates the first murder. The loan shark is lured into the alley, where Sean intends to kill him with his bare hands. Once he sees him he has second thoughts about his capacity to do this, and picks up a brick and batters the loan shark to death. DS Giggs is enticed to Tina's flat which has been covered in black plastic sheeting to prevent mess. Once the murder has been committed, Giggs is wrapped up in the black sheeting, and his body is taken to some waste ground and dumped. Sean and Tina taunt the police by sending a video, which is typical of the organised killer's belief in his own superiority. It is this belief that results in Tina's capture; she thinks she can outwit Fitz and entrap him in the same way as Giggs. Fitz sees through her cover story and guesses that she must be one of the murderers.

The killer of the young schoolboy in *One Day a Lemming Will Fly* was also organised. Whoever it was had gone out that night to kill, because he had brought the rope to hang the boy with him. Cassidy, the school teacher, whom Fitz suspects would clearly fit the bill as far as organisational skills were concerned. The mistake Fitz makes is to assume that the killing was a crime of passion on Cassidy's part, rather than the boy being the physical representation of a fantasy to a stranger. It is an understandable mistake for Fitz to make because there hadn't been any similar crimes with which to link it. But Cassidy's innocence is bad news for both Fitz and Bilborough, not just because they have been instrumental in putting the wrong man behind bars, but because it is almost certain, given the nature of the first offence, that there will be others to follow.

One of the best examples of a real life organised killer is Denis Nilsen, one of Britain's more notorious serial killers. Nilsen was a low ranking civil servant, to whom nobody ever paid much attention, who murdered 15 boys at his home in Cricklewood, London. He would go out trawling for young boys, who had either run away from home or were established rent boys, in the pubs and clubs of Soho where sleaze was a way of life and anonymity guaranteed. Having found a likely victim Nilsen would take him home, have sex with him, kill him, and frequently, he would then practise necrophilia. Once Nilsen's fantasies with a particular body had been exhausted, he would dismember it, and frequently dispose of it by flushing the remains down the lavatory. He was only caught when neighbours complained about the smell coming from a blocked drain; when it was cleared, the human remains were found.

One of the reasons Nilsen went uncaught for so long was because his victims went unnoticed and no one knew they were dead. Missing runaway teenage boys aren't a high priority for the police; the young boys who hang out in the West End of London are part of a strange, amorphous, transient sub-culture where people come and go all the time, and unless there are obvious grounds for suspicion a disappearance here and there is of no great concern to anyone. Nilsen understood this culture perfectly, and chose his victims with great care. Once he had enticed a boy back to his flat, he was almost bound to be able to get away with murder providing he disposed of the bodies in the right way.

Given this, perhaps a more interesting question than 'Why did it take so long to catch Denis Nilsen?' is 'Why was he caught at all?' Nilsen knew that no one had missed any of the boys, so why, towards the end of the killings did he fail to pay the same attention to the disposal of the bodies as he had at the beginning? Whatever else Nilsen may have been he wasn't stupid, and it must have occurred to him that if he was having trouble flushing the remains down the lavatory then the drains must get blocked, and once that happened he would be caught. One answer comes immediately to mind; that his fantasies had completely taken over to the point where he had lost touch with reality. This is possible, but Nilsen's actions on the day he was caught suggest a further explanation. The drains were being investigated as he left for work in the morning, and even though he must have known that he would shortly be arrested, he went off to work as normal, did a full day's work, and returned home - where he was promptly arrested. At no time did he try to escape. His colleagues at work reported that he seemed quite normal, which might indicate that he wasn't completely deluded. Perhaps the answer is that some organised killers who have created a web of ever more complex fantasies find that at some point their fantasies fail to satisfy them in the way for which they long. Just as an alcoholic can sometimes find that he is sick to death of his compulsion to drink, perhaps an organised killer can find that he is sick of his murderous fantasies and subconsciously, or even consciously, leaves clues which can lead to his arrest.

A serial killer whose actions would tend to give credence to this hypothesis is the American, Edmund Kemper, a 6ft 9in, 20 stone, not-so-gentle giant who committed a string of murders in California in the early '70s. From the age of ten, Kemper had fantasies about killing his mother, who used to constantly mock him. His mother divorced his father and then got remarried twice more before he was 14, and during one period of marital difficulty Kemper was sent to live with his grandparents. His grandmother treated him with the same contempt as his mother, and one afternoon he crept up behind her and shot her. Not wanting his grandfather to find his wife dead, he shot him too.

As a result of these crimes Kemper was sent to a mental hospital, and was released into his mother's care five years later in 1970, apparently fully fit and well. Less than two years later, after a row with his mother, he killed again - this time the victim was a young woman. Over the course of the next year or so Kemper killed eight more women, and the nature of the crimes show a clear progression in his fantasy. Initially the victims were killed and dumped, but as the fantasy developed he began not only to take them back to his flat but also to mutilate, dismember, and perform acts of necrophilia with them. Later on he would go further still by taking his victims in the boot of the car to his mother's house and place parts of their bodies in her house and remove them a short while later. His *piece de resistance* was to bury one of his victim's heads beneath his mother's bedroom window. Kemper's killings ended when he killed his mother in the way he had fantasized at the age of ten - by clubbing her to death with a hammer. Later that afternoon, having invited his mother's best friend to the house, he killed her, too, and went to sleep on his mother's bed. Next morning he went to a public call box, phoned the police, and confessed to all his crimes.

Kemper's murders prompt the rather flip thought that it would have been a great deal better for everyone involved if he had just got on with killing his mother first, because the progression of his actions clearly demonstrates that she was the object both of his fantasies and his hatred. Yet Kemper's case does provoke a more serious response and bears comparison with Denis Nilsen. Kemper's behaviour during the killings betrays a certain confusion. On the one hand he was very good at killing, and evading capture. He showed the capacity to learn from mistakes he had made in his murders, and even had the presence of mind to talk his way past two security guards when he was leaving a university campus with two of his victims still alive and groaning in the back of his car. And yet despite his highly disciplined approach, Kemper began to make mistakes. His car picked up a bullet hole in the course of his shootings, the boot became so blood soaked that it became impossible to clean properly, and he went out and bought a new gun that he didn't need, thereby bringing himself to the attention of the police who remembered his conviction for the killings of his grandparents. In fact none of these errors attracted police suspicion, but he later admitted that it was the fear they might that led him to kill his mother at the time he did, and to give himself up thereafter.

Kemper's fantasies had a clear shelf life as far as he was concerned because once their cycle was complete he surrendered himself to the police. Is it not possible then that the reason behind his allowing errors - that only he could perceive - into his actions was the way he acknowledged to himself that his fantasies were no longer giving him what he wanted and impelled him to bring them to a close. Of course this insight does not make an organised killer a safer individual than imagined, because there is always the possibility that another, different, fantasy might begin. However if this insight is valid then it does have some implications for offender profiling. The common assumption has always been that it is the earliest crimes in any sequence that will provide the most psychological clues to the perpetrator. This may still be so, but if the fantasy development of the organised killer has, in some cases, an inbuilt life span which the offender at some level accepts and leaves clues to indicate this, then perhaps there is more to be read and learned from the later crime scenes than has hitherto been imagined. The secret for the profiler is, as ever, to recognise what those clues are and to interpret them correctly.

*   *   *   *

Despite its success in the United States, the British police took a long time to accept the effectiveness of offender profiling, and as a result it only gained acceptance in this country in the mid to late 1980s. In some ways this was deeply ironic because profiling is probably better suited to Britain rather than America. Britain is a much smaller country with a more homogeneous society which theoretically makes profiling easier because patterns will tend to be more consistent. In America murder is a state rather than federal offence which means that the FBI are not automatically called in to investigate. Consequently, it is possible that a number of murders can be committed in different states without anyone making the connection between them. Likewise, even when the FBI are called in they cannot be certain whether there are any other linked crimes that have yet to be discovered. Of course there will always be an element of doubt about this for the British police too, but since information is far more centralised in this country, the likelihood is far smaller.

Good profiling depends on good information. Computerisation has helped on both sides of the Atlantic: the FBI started a National Centre for Violent Crime Analysis where it was proposed to keep a register of all violent crimes and criminals, while the growth of police computer networks in Britain meant that information that was previously only available on card-indexes in each police station was now accessible nationwide. Even so, logic dictates that the quality of information open to police and psychologists in Britain must be superior to that in America. A computer programme is only as good as the data it holds, and given the difference in size - both of area and population - between the two countries, the smaller country is likely to have a more complete record. Indeed, profiling and computers have gone hand in hand with one another ever since profiling began to play a mainstream role in British police investigations, and there are those who argue that it is only the computer that has given profiling a scientific status.

It was in 1986 that profiling became front page news in Britain with the arrest of John Duffy, the 'Railway Rapist', thanks largely to the involvement of David Canter, a professor of psychology at Guildford University. Canter had never heard of the FBI's work in criminal profiling when he was invited to lunch at Scotland Yard in 1985 to discuss ways in which behavioural psychology might help a police investigation, and it was quite by chance that he became involved in the Duffy case. Two months after this first meeting with the police, he was travelling home to Guildford by train when his eye caught a story in the *London Evening Standard* about a series of 24 sexual assaults, all of which took place near railway lines and all involving the same attacker, though sometimes he had an accomplice. Canter decided to see if he could detect any obvious patterns.

He drew up a list of the times and dates of the assaults, and inferred that it was only recently that the attacker had begun to strike on his own and speculated on what this might say about the relationship between the two attackers. He committed his thoughts to paper and sent them to the police, and several months later was asked back to Hendon Police College. Unknown to David Canter, the police had now forensically linked the rapes to the murders of Alison Day, a 19-year-old secretary, in December 1985 in Hackney, and Maartje Tamboezer, a 15-year-old school girl, in early 1986 in a wood near Guildford. The rape enquiry was now a full-scale murder enquiry, and Professor Canter was asked to assist the enquiry on an official basis, and was given two serving police officers, Rupert Heritage and Jim Blann, to help him.

This request marked a sea change in police attitudes to seeking outside help, but it put David Canter in something of a quandary. By now he had read some of the material on offender profiling to come out of Quantico, but although it contained much helpful information, there was no 'Do-It-Yourself' Guide on how to compile a profile. Canter's first attempt at a profile would be largely a matter of trial and error - a nerve-wracking experience in a 'live' investigation.

Canter and his two assistants began to analyze all the actions in the different crimes - how the victims were approached, how he spoke to them, what threats he made etc. They soon realized that although many of the victims varied greatly in their descriptions of the lone attacker, the character of the assaults was totally consistent with the same man being involved each time, and moreover indicated that he was steadily gaining in confidence. They were beginning to form an impression of the killer from the way he related to his victims, when a third body was found. The remains of Anne Locke, a 30-year-old secretary, were discovered in a field in Hertfordshire in July 1986; the binding of the fingers and the attempts to set it in fire had all the hallmarks of the 'Railway Rapist'.

Seven days after the third body was found, Professor Canter presented his preliminary profile to the police. The suspect would be in his mid to late 20s; he would have lived within the area of the first three attacks since 1983, and would possibly have been under arrest sometime between October 1983 and January 1984, though not necessarily for a sex-related crime. He would probably be married or have a girl-friend, though the relationship was likely to be in difficulties. His job would not bring him into close contact with the general public, and would be skilled or semi-skilled, involving weekend work or casual labour from about June 1994. He would keep himself to himself but would have a couple of close men friends. He would have little or no contact with women on a daily basis, though the variety of the sexual actions during his assaults would indicate a wide sexual experience. He would have a sound knowledge of the railway system along which the attacks occurred.

So how did Professor Canter make these assumptions? Most rapes are committed by men in their late teens or early twenties, but because of the planning and the varied locations involved, these assaults suggested an older man. An analysis of the chronology of the attacks showed an ever widening circle from the first three which all took place in close proximity to one another. Canter examined the crimes closely and saw that whereas by the end of the series of rapes the rapist had progressed to murder, at the beginning he was almost mindful of his victim's feelings. This suggested that the early assaults might have started out as something of an experiment, and that the rapist would have found his victims at random close to home. It was only as he became more criminally sophisticated and confident that the attacks spread out over a wider area.

The lull in attacks between October 1983 and January 1984 was grounds for thinking that the rapist had been forced to call a temporary halt to his activities. Given the increased forensic awareness that he showed thereafter - in the form of combing the pubic hair, wiping his victims with tissue and then setting fire to the tissues etc - it was reasonable to conclude that the hiatus in his crimes was precipitated by an arrest. The rapist was able to control and channel his violence when engaged in his sexual assaults, and so the offence for which he was arrested was unlikely to be of a sexual nature. He never stole from his victims and so burglary or theft were again unlikely, and the most probable cause for his arrest would have been an outbreak of violence that he did not consider to be criminal behaviour.

The rapist used his social skills to attract his victims, and at times, even during an assault, could appear to show compassion for his victims by asking them if they were OK, and giving them advice on the best way to get home. Such behaviour indicated a man who was used to being in a relationship with a woman, though the violent, controlling side of his nature which was also apparent in the attacks, suggested that he would not be capable of maintaining any relationship for a prolonged period of time.

The latently violent nature of the rapist made it unlikely that he would be unable to hold down a job which brought him into daily contact with the public, especially women, but the degree of planning that went into each attack was the work of a man with a skilled or at least semi-skilled job. Most rapists will commit their crimes in a way that does not draw attention to themselves, and so the random timings of the assaults was consistent with either shift or part-time work, because the attacker would have used the alibi and anonymity that his working environment provided to minimise the risk of getting caught. The fact that so many attacks took place near railway lines or stations and that the attacker often told his victims the quickest way home by train was clear evidence of a man with a sound working knowledge of the railway network in and around London.

A few months later, in November 1986, John Duffy was arrested for the murder of the three women and a number of rapes, and shortly afterwards David Canter was telephoned by the police to say that the profile he had provided had proved extremely accurate and had been of great value to the investigation. Duffy was one of 2000 suspects that the police had identified. He had made it on to the list, because he had once raped his wife at knife-point after she had walked out on him. Even so, Duffy was only number 1505 on the list of suspects because the police had treated the attack on his wife as a domestic assault, and had failed to make the connection that a man who did this to his wife was capable of doing it to another woman. However, Duffy was one of only a few suspects to match the profile closely, and the only one to live in the Kilburn area predicted. Duffy was put under surveillance for two weeks, and the police became convinced that they had found their man. He was later convicted for the three murders and five rapes.

Professor Canter and his two colleagues had made the almost perfect profile. Not only did Duffy live in the area predicted, and was separated from his wife who left him in 1985 to get away from his violence and excessive sexual demands. He had been convicted of raping his wife and beating up her new boy-friend. After the attack on his wife he had been forensically examined by the police, which had taught him how to minimize the evidence left behind at the scene of the crimes. His occupation fitted the profile better than any psychologist could have dared to hope; Duffy was a travelling carpenter for British Rail.

The only answer that the profile failed to provide was why Duffy started to kill. What made him make the transition from successful rapist to killer? Professor Canter had realized that understanding this change of behaviour would be a clear pointer to who the suspect was, but was unable to draw any inferences from the data to hand. The explanation only came to light after Duffy was caught. His fifth rape victim was taken to Hendon magistrates court in December 1985, where Duffy was facing an assault charge brought by his wife. His victim failed to identify him, but, as she stared at him, he recognised her, and he decided there and then that allowing his victims to live was too risky. Any further women he raped would have to be killed. Alison Day was killed within a month of Duffy's appearance in court.

The John Duffy case has two parallels with 'Mad Woman in the Attic', the first *Cracker* story. The most obvious is that they both have a railway theme, but much less so, because what wasn't widely reported at the time, is that amnesia played a key role in the Duffy investigation. Unlike the monk in *Mad Woman in the Attic*, though, who has a genuine case of amnesia and desperately wants to recover his memory, there is every reason to believe Duffy is faking the amnesia he has claimed concerning all his actions around the time of the rapes and murders. After being interviewed by the police in connection with the attacks on his wife, he tottered into a nearby police station badly wounded, declaring that he had been beaten up and had lost his memory. He was so convincing that he was admitted to a psychiatric hospital for this condition. A friend of Duffy's later admitted that he had attacked Duffy at his own request, because Duffy had wanted an excuse to fake amnesia. As we know, Jimmy McGovern had held on to the idea for *Mad Woman in the Attic* ever since he watched *The Fugitive* on TV as a kid, and even if he had heard of the 'Railway Rapist', he certainly had never heard of the details about his amnesia. So the links between the real life horror of John Duffy's crimes and the TV drama of Cracker are no more than coincidence, but what a field day a psychologist would have with them. After all, what were the odds of the first ever large scale British criminal investigation in which offender profiling played a significant role, and the first story of the first prime time British TV drama to feature a forensic psychologist as hero, both containing railways and suspects accused of amnesia?

Despite his triumph of logic in the Duffy enquiry,

Professor Canter was still far from clear as to whether his success was a one-off or whether it formed the basis for a genuine scientific analysis. His understanding of the American literature on profiling, reinforced by a visit to the Behavioural Science Unit at Quantico, had left him with the impression that the Americans had gathered together an immense amount of material about serial killers and rapists, but in any given investigation their forensic psychologists would compile their profiles on intuition and insight based on their own knowledge and experience. This had produced some tremendous results, but Canter, a computer expert with something of a passion for number-crunching, was concerned about the academic rigour of a behavioural psychology that relied so much on intuition. As he wrote in his book 'Criminal Shadows', 'science is the development of theories, generalizable principles, and the testing of them against reliable facts......Assumptions and conjectures may be the first steps in the emergence of scientific explanations, but they fizzle out if they are not consistently supported by the solid fuel of data'. Canter thought that assumptions and conjectures were as far as the Americans had got with profiling, and he set out to provide the facts to turn it into a science.

Canter started to analyze data of past crimes about which information was known by looking at every action in detail and classifying it accordingly, and correlating it to what was known about the offender. By so doing he was building up a data base which would establish a quantifiable probable relationship between any future crime of a particular sort and the likely offender. Canter still has a long way to go to produce a watertight unified theory of criminal behaviour, but one area in which he has made notable progress is in criminal mapping in rape enquiries.

The most significant aspect of the Duffy enquiry for Professor Canter had been his observation that the first crimes had been committed near to where Duffy lived. This dovetailed neatly with Robert Ressler's idea that the first crimes gave the most clues to an offender's identity, and Canter was intrigued as to whether other criminals started their careers so close to home. His initial enquiries centred on burglaries, and the findings were so astonishing that they became the basis of his 'circle hypothesis'. Studies of burglaries known, or believed, to be committed by the same person, showed that the crimes were all spread over a surprisingly local area, and that in 80% of the cases the offender lived within the circle defined by the crimes. This information has had a profound effect on the way that the police deploys its resources. Northumbrian police have monitored areas where burglary is rampant, and can now predict where and when the next spate of burglaries is likely to take place, and can increase police surveillance of those areas without having to worry about under-manning in other potential hot spots.

The circle hypothesis also proved remarkably reliable in an analysis of serial killers. When Dr Canter plotted the locations of 'Jack the Ripper's' four victims in Whitechapel, he found that the two men who are commonly believed to have committed the murders, Aaron Kosminski and James Maybrick, both had residences well within the circle defined by the murder locations. It is thought that Kosminski lived close to his brother at the very heart of the circle, and that Maybrick, although primarily resident in Liverpool, had a London base in Whitechapel. Further analysis would suggest that Kosminski was the most likely suspect, because most offences are committed from a permanent rather than a temporary base. The crime scenes of the other 'Ripper', the 'Yorkshire Ripper', also revealed something similar. Indeed in 1980 Stuart Kind, a Home Office scientist working on the enquiry, pointed out that if the killer was to live at the epicentre of the crimes he would be residing near Bradford. Kind had inadvertently stumbled on the circle hypothesis without even realizing it, but because its importance was not understood at the time, the police paid no attention to it.

Aside from initially concentrating any investigation close to a crime scene, what Professor Canter deduced from these findings was that just as every law-abiding citizen has his or her own mental map of familiar locations, so too do offenders. Ordinary people will define their surroundings by the journeys they make - to the shops, school, parents etc, and the further away they get from the familiar the less safe they feel. Likewise a criminal will have a mental map of locations, usually close to home, that will represent a territory on which he feels safe to offend. Therefore the location of any crime scene is a vital pointer to the offender. If the forensic psychologist can understand what a particular location is likely to mean to an offender, he is more than half-way to identifying him.

The case of the 'Tower Block Rapist' provides a fine illustration of this point. Between 1986 and 1988 in the Edgbaston area of Birmingham there were eight cases of old women in their seventies and eighties being threatened at knife-point in their high-rise flats, and then being taken to the roof of the tower block and raped. The police were baffled at how someone could get away with so many crimes in a public place in broad daylight and their enquiry had produced no suspects when Professor Canter was asked to help. Canter quickly realized that the suspect would most likely live in a tower block, because only someone who had that experience would instinctively feel safe in that environment. Whereas the police might think there was a high probability of getting caught taking an old lady on to the roof, a tower block resident would know how truly anonymous such buildings are. Recognising that the offender would be unlikely to live in one of the tower blocks where the crimes were committed, Canter predicted that the suspect would live in the tower block in the Highgate area, just across the road from the scene of the first four rapes. Canter understood that the dual carriageways that cut through Birmingham create mental as well as physical boundaries, and that the road would divide one community from the other; the suspect would have been able to go about his daily business with little fear of being recognised by one of his victims, despite living in such close proximity. Adrian Babb went to court in 1989 and was convicted of three rapes with another four taken into consideration; he had been living in a tower block in the Highgate area at the time of the offences.

A great deal more is understood about the motivations and actions of rapists than serial killers today; extensive research into rape has been done by psychologists of all persuasions over the years, but even so Professor Canter has made his mark with his understanding of the mental geography of offenders in this field, too. The difference between those men who rape indoors and those outdoors had long been recognised, but while many correct inferences had been made about the different types of men involved, there was little by way of concrete explanation for how a rapist initially came to choose one scene or the other. Criminals tend to choose the same crime scene regardless of the crime, because it is the environment in which they feel comfortable. A burglar who progresses to rape is likely to do so indoors, where someone who rapes outdoors is more likely to come from a background of indecent assault or street crime.

While these observations tied in with Professor Canter's theories of criminal maps, they were still extremely crude because, while stating a general truth, there was a wide margin of discrepancy. Not every indoor rapist committed his offences in the same way, and not every outdoor rapist had no convictions for burglary. In order to highlight the more subtle distinctions, Canter analyzed a series of rapes and broke down each crime into its component parts - how much violence was involved, what sexual activity took place etc. Thirty-one different actions were fed into a computer to be matched for the likelihood of co-occurrence; the results showed that while there were some actions - surprise attack, removing the victim's clothes, and vaginal penetration that were common to all rapes, other actions and sexual activities separated into three distinct clusters, which indicated there were three different types of rapist. Canter classified these types as follows: the rapist who treats his victim as an object - such a man is close to the popular conception of a psychopath, having little idea of how other people feel. The rapist for whom the victim is a vehicle - such a man recognises how human relationships work but has no emotional contact with that understanding and his victims are merely people to help him fulfil his fantasies. Lastly there is the rapist who treats his victims as a person - such a man is the closest to a 'normal' human being of the three.

This may all sound rather technical and academic, but it

important part of the criminal psycholo-
Ian Stephen says: 'Whenever a new mur-
on the radio or TV, I get a gut feeling about
ng to a few details, I can almost invariably tell
omestic incident, a gangland killing, or a ser-
make predictions in my head about what type
police should be looking for.' Whether profil-
ecome wholly scientific remains to be seen, but
tainly be one person who will be delighted if it
Can you imagine Fitz tied to a computer screen?

has a practical usage. It has created extra categories apart from 'organised' and 'disorganised' by which to interpret patterns of crime, and in one famous case it helped the police to solve a series of ten rapes in the Midlands in 1988. Although there was no direct forensic evidence to connect the assaults, there were sufficient similarities for the police to believe that all the rapes had been committed by the same person. All the victims were women students in rented accommodation who were attacked while sleeping alone, and on each occasion the assailant was black. What is more, apart from on the first occasion which might just have been an experiment and on the sixth when he was disturbed, the attacker always asked the victim for help in achieving penetration.

Professor Canter was called into the investigation in 1989. He, too, initially assumed that the rapes had been committed by the same person, but as he studied the evidence it began to dawn on him that there might be two attackers involved. While consistently asking for help with penetration might seem damning evidence of just one assailant, there were no statistics to prove it. If asking for such help was quite common during a rape, then it would be no pointer to anyone in particular. However, while the range of sexual activities and levels of violence might suggest an attacker that was growing in confidence, evidence from solved cases suggested that a rapist who reassured and fondled his victims was unlikely to be capable of a masked, violent attack.

Before Professor Canter had fully determined whether two offenders were involved, forensic scientists settled the matter for him by detecting two different strands of DNA in samples left behind by the attackers. However, there was still the small matter of identifying the assailants. Canter and his team began to analyze the crimes in still greater behavioural detail, and were able to attribute each crime to a particular attacker. Those of the rapist who saw his victims as people were labelled the work of the 'Wimp', and those of the rapist who saw his victims as objects they called the work of 'Macho Man'. Working on expected life and behaviour patterns of each type of rapist, and drawing a circle around each set of rapes, Canter drew up a profile of the attackers and predicted where they might live. In June 1989 two men were arrested and later received long prison sentences for their part in the rapes. Both conformed to the profile that Professor Canter had drawn up, and lived within the area predicted.

Offender profiling has by no means been one man's preserve in this country. Dr Paul Britton has also contributed significantly to some prominent police investigations. He produced a stunningly accurate portrait of Michael Sams after the murder of Julie Dart. Sams, he said, would be in his late 40s to early 50s, would be familiar with electric tools and machinery though not a senior employee in an organisation, would make contact with the police, and would re-offend. Britton was right in all these predictions, but unfortunately Sams was not caught until after Stephanie Slater had been abducted and imprisoned. He helped to negotiate Stephanie's release, and was on hand at Sams' trial to advise the prosecution counsel. It was also Paul Britton's advice that the police look for an ex-policeman in the baby foods contamination enquiry, that resulted in the conviction of Detective Sergeant Rodney Whitchelo.

Offender profiling has justifiably grabbed the public's attention: while it is true that most murders and rapes are solved by more conventional police work, forensic psycholo-

gy has helped to cr____ _____
trable cases. _____
early days for _____
crucial moral an_____
to answer. It has b_____
on profiling will ena_____
police by acting in an_____
tively minor worry; psy_____
iour and thought pattern_____
inal to act out of character_____

More worrying is that _____
brought in for questioning w_____
merely because they fit a profi_____
guilty, but refuses to confess, the p_____
go, and there is a known correlation_____
ing up to murder after their release fr_____
cumstances should a suspect be brough_____
he isn't might he not re-offend anyway?_____

Despite the efforts of Robert Ressler _____
offender profiling is still far from being _____
Indeed, one gender has so far been largely ig_____
the modern research has been focused on men, _____
always widely held that women don't become s_____
Recent evidence contradicts this somewhat. C_____
Missen, a postgraduate student in Professor Cant_____
department has compiled an exhaustive list of Britisl_____
killers over the last one hundred years. There have been_____
in all, of which 20 have been women.

There is still a great deal to be discovered and understoo_____
about how serial killers think and behave before offender pro_____
filing becomes truly scientific, and so insight and intuition

CHAPTER 5

THE IRRESISTABLE RISE
OF THE SCREEN DETECTIVE

'PSYCHOLOGY IS THE religion of the late twentieth century in Western culture. Discuss.' This is just the sort of clever-dick throwaway remark one can imagine Fitz making to provoke some students, or better still, to belittle and irritate DS Beck, but it is also one that bears some examination when trying to account for the phenomenal success of *Cracker*. After all, it's not every day that a series with a psychologist as the central character becomes an instant hit. Of course, superb scripts, high production values, and strong acting, all played a major role in this, but there was something over and beyond these qualities that captured the imagination of critics and viewers alike.

Few people would disagree that Western society has become more secular; what is open to debate is why. An old-fashioned Marxist of the 'Religion is the opium of the masses' school might contend that people have wised up to the church as an arm of the state's control, while a more mainstream analyst might point to a disillusionment with the increasing disparity between doctrine and practice. Whatever your viewpoint, what seems incontrovertible is that at the very least many people are no longer getting the good feelings that they associated with religious belief. This doesn't mean that God is dead, or that Eastern religions are inherently superior to their Western counterparts, but that, as Dario Fo, the Italian playwright, once said: 'People are leaving the churches to find God'.

Part of the value of a religious belief lies in the sense of security that it gives to the person who holds it. There is a clearly prescribed moral and spiritual code for this life, and the freedom from anxiety from life's great unknown - death - through the promise of an afterlife. In an uncertain world, religion should provide some certainty and meaning, but in a century which has seen two world wars, the Holocaust, Stalin's purges, countless minor wars, rising crime levels, widespread political corruption, and where the bad guys often seem to get away with it, it is perhaps not surprising that people are no longer finding the reassurance they seek in the traditional organized religions.

Yet the need for reassurance still exists, and if people don't get it from religion they will go elsewhere. Sigmund Freud, the father of psychoanalysis, considers religious fervour as a desire to reproduce the 'oceanic feeling' of archaic bliss. This is felt by an infant when he has a sense of absolute security in the arms of his mother. The adult seeks a similar protection against external forces in the form of religion, just as the child longs for a parent to comfort him in his helplessness. This may seem a little far-fetched to some, but the prevalence of the Madonna and Child in western religious iconography makes one wonder whether Freud had a point.

Regardless of the rights and wrongs of Freud, it is undeniable that even if people haven't abandoned religion entirely, they have certainly looked for other ways to top up their need for a sense of meaning to their lives. For many, the quest for money, power, and status has a quasi-religious fervour. We shall never know - in this life at least! - whether Robert Maxwell's greed and corruption has taken him to the kingdom of heaven, but we do know that it has taken him to the cemetery on the Mount of Olives, the holiest burial place in the Jewish world.

However, nothing has stepped quite so easily into the vacuum created by the failure of the established church as psychology. Since people and countries have long since stopped behaving along lines which orthodox religions dictate they ought, a science, or pseudo-science as some might say, which looks at what people actually do, and why they do it, becomes immensely seductive. To put it more crudely still, when a world with a God at its centre fails to give the hoped for sense of security, it is small wonder that people turn for reassurance to something they believe helps to understand both themselves and how they operate within the world.

Religion and psychology have some marked parallels. Both offer a wide variety of traditions. If the Church of England doesn't give you what you're looking for, there's everything from Catholicism to Seventh Day Adventism to choose from. Similarly, psychologists, therapists, and counsellors come in all shapes and persuasions. If you want some old-fashioned analysis you can see a Freudian and lie on a couch five times a week; if you want something more 1990s you might see a cognitive therapist, while if you're after something a bit wacky you might try lying under a pyramid, à la Fergie.

Likewise, the sense of belonging to a religious or psychological tradition confers a sense of exclusivity. Not only are you supplied with a belief system, but you get your own language thrown in. Religions often adopt their own calendar, and those in the psychological know can use terms like 'gestalt' and 'child within' in the certain knowledge that they are almost meaningless to anyone who isn't 'in the know'. What is more, just as religions need priests to interpret the word of God, so the individual requires a psychologist for an interpretation of himself.

So where does *Cracker* fit into all this? Different genres of fiction appeal to diverse sections of the population in various cultures. For instance, in Britain, *Mills & Boon* romances are largely read by women - presumably because they are most in need of the romantic escapism they provide. In India, the most avid readers are men. The idea of thousands of Indian men sitting on Bombay railway station reading: 'Marjorie suddenly realized that something magical was happening; this time it was for ever,' conjures a wonderful comic image, but it isn't as absurd as it first seems, as Robbie Coltrane points out. 'Arranged marriages are still relatively commonplace, and many men dream of being able to marry for love. The *Mills & Boon* romances provide an outlet for these feelings.'

Given this, one has to look a little deeper than the literary skills of detective writers, accomplished as they often are, for the popularity of this genre in Britain and the USA over the last hundred years or so. Detective stories solve those moral dilemmas that just aren't solved in real life. How often did you say as a child: 'That's not fair' only to get the predictable adult reply: 'Life isn't fair'? Well, more often than not, detective stories are fair. There's good and there's bad, and the bad gets caught. All of which is much more reassuring than being told: 'The meek shall inherit the earth' while some Serbian psychopath is doing his best to commit genocide. When, as with *Cracker*, you introduce a psychologist as the detective, you have a very powerful cocktail indeed.

Detective fiction has always had a psychological basis of some sort, because all crimes have to have some motive, but more often than not it has taken a back seat to the narrative demands of the whodunit. One might be able to make a claim for Sherlock Holmes as the first fictional behavioral forensic psychologist in that on one occasion he was able to solve a murder without attending the scene of crime, but his more usual *modus operandi* was to find the villain through a process of deduction after a careful examination of the evidence. It has only been comparatively recently, as psychology has become better understood and more widely accepted, that detective fiction, most notably in the novels of Ruth Rendell and PD James, has given fuller weight to the psychological motivation of its characters. As psychology has grown into an established science, so detective fiction has matured with it, and the development of forensic psychology, and in particular offender profiling, has provided a further dimension still, as the success of *Silence of the Lambs* well demonstrates. With psychologists and police working side by side, detective writers are freer than ever to focus on the motive and how it comes to be understood, which, after all, is the main point of interest - the emotional heart - of any crime story.

Fitz is very much a 1990s' - almost post-modern - hero. He drinks too much, he gambles, he's politically incorrect, he's eclectic in his influences, he's clever, and he's gifted with penetrating insight into others whilst having very little into himself. Yet no matter how contemporary Fitz appears, there's no doubting that he's firmly located within the pantheon of fictional maverick detective heroes. Indeed, by some standards Fitz might even appear quite conventional. Take the opening of the Sherlock Holmes story, *The Sign of Four*, as an example:-

'*Sherlock Holmes took his bottle from the corner of the mantelpiece, and his hypodermic syringe from its neat Morocco case. With his long, white, nervous fingers he adjusted the delicate needle, and rolled back his left shirt-cuff. For some little time his eyes rested thoughtfully upon the sinewy forearm and wrist, all dotted and scarred with innumerable puncture marks. Finally, he thrust the sharp point home, pressed down the tiny piston, and sank back into the velvet-lined armchair with a long sigh of satisfaction.*

"*Which is it today,*" *I asked,* "*morphine or cocaine?*"

He raised his eyes languidly from the old black letter volume which he had opened.

"*It is cocaine,*" *he said,* "*a seven per cent solution. Would you care to try it?*" '

This reads more like a Will Self novel than a detective classic of the nineteenth century. No one would even dream of giving a popular prime-time character such questionable traits these days. Can you imagine Fitz or Morse having to stop for a quick fix? I don't think so.

However, if you were to substitute alcohol and gambling for cocaine and morphine, then Sherlock Holmes and Fitz aren't so very far apart. Indeed all the great detectives have so much in common that one can create a psychological profile for them, in much the same way as forensic psychologists do for offenders. The first detective novel is generally held to be Wilkie Collin's *The Moonstone*, and its hero, Sergeant Cuff set the benchmark by which all later detectives would be judged.

The first description that we get of him is:-

'A grizzled elderly man, so miserably lean that he looked as if he had not got an ounce of flesh on his bones in any part of him. He was dressed all in decent black, with a white cravat around his neck. His face was as sharp as a hatchet, and the skin of it was as yellow and dry and withered as an autumn leaf. His eyes, of a steely light grey, had a very disconcerting trick when they encountered your eyes, of looking as if they expected something more from you than you were aware of yourself. His walk was soft; his voice was melancholy; his long lanky fingers were hooked like claws. He might have been a parson, or an undertaker - or anything else you like, except what he really was.'

Sergeant Cuff is immediately established as being out of the ordinary, and this outsider status is confirmed by the fact he isn't local. We soon learn, though, that his rather forbidding exterior hides some very human qualities, such as a dry sense of humour and a passion for rose growing. In short, he's every inch the hero.

The next great detective was probably the most famous of them all, Sherlock Holmes. Like Sergeant Cuff, Holmes too is a loner, but unlike him, Holmes has a sidekick, Dr Watson, with whom he shares lodgings in Baker St. He has a fondness for narcotics, smoking a pipe, atonal violin, long bursts of inactivity followed by hyperactivity, and dressing up, all of which help to personalize his almost superhuman intelligence.

Other detectives follow in the same mould. Hercule Poirot, Miss Marple, Philip Marlowe, and Inspector Morse are all outsiders. Except for Philip Marlowe they all have sidekicks: Poirot has Hastings, Miss Marple has her nephew Raymond, and Morse has Sergeant Lewis. What is more, they all have their eccentricities. If being Belgian wasn't enough, Poirot is the anal retentive par excellence. Miss Marple has the audacity not only to be a woman, but a granny to boot. Marlowe has a weakness for the booze, and Morse has a passion for real ale, opera, and Mark 2 Jags.

So what would a psychological profile for Fitz, as the latest in a long tradition of popular detective heroes, suggest? He should be white, male, intelligent, unmarried or on the verge of separation, with some weakness that makes him in need of redemption, without ever appearing irredeemable. It is this last point that will surely stop Hannibal Lecter ever entering the detective Hall of Fame. He's a wonderful character with a brilliant mind who points Clarice Starling towards the serial killer, but ultimately he's just too beyond the pale for the reader to care about.

Of course, Fitz fits the bill fairly accurately, as in many ways he was bound to, because fiction and drama thrive on conflict rather than harmony. As Robbie Coltrane points out: 'If the blurb for the next series ran, "Fitz and Judith go to Habitat to buy two Yucca plants and a new coffee table, and then go home to discuss their summer holidays with Mark and Katy," then no one would bother to switch on their TV.'

Yet it would be wrong to imagine that Fitz's success as a detective hero depends on his fulfilling the criteria of a psychological profile, for there have been countless other fictional heros who have done so and have disappeared into obscurity. In the same way that offender profiling only points to the type of person who would be likely to have committed a particular crime, the profile of fictional detectives can only predict the bare bones, and not the flesh and blood, of a character. A fictional hero stands or falls not on the ingenuity of his solutions or his character, but on his ability to grab the heart and mind of his audience.

Certainly Fitz's drinking, gambling, intelligence, and chaotic personal life, all help to engage the viewer, but perhaps his greatest asset is in the way he doesn't conform to a typical profile. Simon Wessely, the senior lecturer in psychological medicine at the Institute of Psychiatry, wrote an article in *The Times*, which preceded the first *Cracker* series, in which he said: 'I have not seen Mr Coltrane's performance as a police psychologist. However, I predict his character will have certain features. He will possess a broad knowledge and intuition. He will also have some character eccentricities, some unusual talents, and may not be the easiest of fellows. He will always get his man.'

But Fitz doesn't always get his man. He sometimes gets it wrong. In the third story of the first series *One Day a Lemming Will Fly*, Fitz is convinced that Cassidy, the school teacher, is guilty of the murder of the young teenaged boy. For virtually the whole story, Fitz piles on the pressure to get Cassidy to confess. Only once he's done so does Fitz realize that he's innocent. By then, Bilborough has already called a press conference which he won't call off, and Fitz has to live with the guilt that he will be partly responsible for sending an innocent man to prison.

Fitz proves he's human. Unlike other detectives who are just as we've always known them at the beginning of each episode or story, Fitz develops. If he's had a row with Judith or Penhaligon at the end of one story, then you know he's going to pay for it in the next. Fitz inhabits a world of confusion and its consequences that we can all understand, while retaining his status as fictional hero. He's fallible enough to remind us of what we really know - that the world is a frightening place about which religion, governments, and psychology don't have all the answers, but he's right enough of the time for us to be reassured and to satisfy our need for wrongdoing to be punished.

Combining psychology with detection has done wonders for police work, and it has done the same for the crime story. No longer is it restricted to the simple narrative demands of who, what, and why, but it can also address the more profound issues such as: 'Does evil exist?' that are at the heart of understanding any crime. In the past we've expected such questions to be answered by religious leaders: now we can expect them to be answered by the psychologist detective. Truly his day has arrived.

Chapter 6

The Storylines

Series One

The Mad Woman In the Attic

The scene is a lecture hall in a northern university, and Fitz is flinging classic psychology and philosophy texts around the room. The students are non-plussed and Fitz is in his element. This is how he likes to see himself: iconoclast, de-bunker of myths, and intellectual anarchist. Later that evening after some heavy losses on the horses, we see the other side of him: pissed, emotionally inarticulate, and unable to cope with his own middle-class lifestyle. Out to dinner with his wife, Judith, and a couple of friends in a local restaurant, he deliberately sets out to be provocative, and the evening ends with water being thrown on his head, and the restaurant refusing his credit card. On their return home, Judith discovers that Fitz has forged her name on a loan document in order to cover his gambling losses; she decides that enough is enough and walks out on him, taking their daughter with her.

The next morning Fitz is sitting idly watching the TV when a news item catches his attention. A young woman whom he used to teach has been found brutally slashed to death on a train, and Fitz becomes determined to help the family of the murdered woman by tracking the killer.

A blood-splattered man, later identified as Kelly, is found lying beside the railway tracks, and immediately becomes the police's prime suspect. On recovering consciousness, Kelly claims complete memory loss, and although the investigating police officers, DCI Bilborough, DS Beck and DS Jane Penhaligon, suspect that the amnesia is faked, they are unable to break his story. Despite circulating his picture in the national press, the only response is a hoax. No one, it seems, knows anything about him.

The police has so far resisted Fitz's pleas for help, but as they get more and more frustrated as their investigations disappear up dead-ends, DCI Bilborough reluctantly decides to let him see what he can do. With DS Penhaligon in attendance, Fitz interviews Kelly for the first time. He tries to make Kelly confess by showing that he identifies with the thought processes that lead to murder, but gets nowhere. At the end of the interrogation Kelly turns to Fitz and says: 'It's you that needs help.'

Despite Fitz's failure to determine whether the amnesia was genuine, DS Penhaligon realizes that Fitz's skills are an asset to the investigation, and when the police are forced - in the absence of a confession or any hard evidence - to let Kelly go, she is instrumental in persuading DCI Bilborough to release him into Fitz's care.

As Fitz and Kelly begin to spend more time together, Kelly begins to recapture flashes of memory, but he still can't piece together the crucial moments. Fitz takes Kelly to the dog-track, and a face in the crowd stirs something in Kelly's mind, and he gives chase but the man escapes him. We later see the same man telephoning the police from Manchester railway station giving the whereabouts of another body and implicating Kelly as the murderer.

The police take this as evidence of Kelly's guilt, but Fitz has now realised that Kelly is psychologically incapable of committing the crimes. In a final interrogation, Kelly's memory comes back. He was on the train; he had caught the real murderer in the act and in the ensuing fight had been thrown off the moving train.

With the collapse of the case against Kelly, the focus switches to two other suspects. One in particular grabs Fitz and Penhaligon's attention. They drive to his home, and once they have been given a false alibi by his father, they known they have the right man. In a race to prevent the suspect from killing again, Fitz finally arrests the man after a chase along the very railway lines where the drama first started.

The story ends with the full return of Kelly's memory. There was no mystery to why nobody came forward to identify him. He was a monk from a closed order with no access to newspapers or TV.

To Say I Love You

Attempts at a reconciliation between Fitz and his wife, Judith, fall apart when Fitz refuses to agree to demands that he should stop gambling. Soon afterwards he is arrested for a breach of the peace outside his in-laws home where Judith and Katie, their daughter are living.

Sean and Tina are a young, unemployed couple living in a high-rise flat. Sean is working-class and has a terrible stutter, while Tina has become estranged from her middle-class family, whom she believes abused her as a child. Tina goes round to visit her family to ask for money, but they refuse to help her as long as she remains with Sean. Angry and frustrated, Sean hi-jacks a bus, and after a short chase is arrested and taken to the same police station where Fitz is being held.

DC Beck interrogates Sean, but makes little headway, and it is only when Fitz is called in that any progress is made. Contrary to Fitz's recommendations, Sean is released on probation. Shortly afterwards Tina lures a loan shark into an alley with a promise of sex, and Sean clubs him to death with a brick.

At the scene of the crime, Fitz gives a graphic demonstration of how the crime was committed while flirting heavily with DS Penhaligon. Later that evening, he appears on a local TV chat show and gives a stunningly accurate profile of the two killers. Sean and Tina are watching the programme at the local bowling alley, and they are panicked into thinking Fitz knows more about them than he really does.

DS Giggs goes to interview Sean and Tina as part of the routine murder enquiries, but they believe the police are on to them. Tina gives Giggs the come-on, and persuades him to come back later that night. Sean and Tina cover their flat in black plastic and video themselves wearing strange masks. When Giggs turns up at the flat, Sean murders him, and together, he and Tina wrap up his body and dump it on waste ground nearby.

Fitz meets up with Judith, who tells him that she will be having dinner with Graham, her therapist, that night. Fitz invites Penhaligon out for a meal to the same restaurant, but once she realises she has been set up for a confrontation, she pours a glass of water over him and walks out. Later on, Fitz and Penhaligon meet up again, and she invites him back to her flat. Just when it seems they might start an affair, Fitz becomes overwhelmed with guilt and leaves.

Sean bumps into Fitz at the police station while signing the probation book, and becomes more convinced than ever that Fitz knows all about him. Sean and Tina then decide that they need to kill Fitz.

Sean and Tina's video is sent to the police, and Fitz immediately recognises Sean. The police rush to the flat but there is no one there. Tina comes into the pub where Fitz is drinking alone, and tries to get him to come home with her. Fitz sees through her and calls the police, and she is arrested.

Fitz and Penhaligon interview Tina and try to get her to tell them Sean's whereabouts. She consistently refuses.

Fitz's private life gets even more confused: Judith wants to come back home, but she confesses to having had an affair with Graham.

Eventually Fitz manages to break Tina's silence. Sean will be going after her blind sister, whom Tina always felt got all the attention at home. The police rush to the family home, but Sean has got there first, and is threatening to blow the house up. After a tense negotiation, Fitz persuades Sean to release Tina's sister, and he himself only just gets out, as the house explodes with Sean still inside.

ONE DAY A LEMMING WILL FLY

A 14 year-old boy named Tim goes missing when he is walking through some local woodlands. He is later found hanging from a tree. His elder brother attacks two fifth formers whom he knew to be bullying Tim, and soon after, Cassidy - Tim's English teacher - makes two unsuccessful attempts to commit suicide.

As Fitz pieces the picture together, it becomes clear that Tim thought he was gay, and had told both his brother and his teacher. Both now feel that they had failed to provide the help that Tim needed, and feel in some way responsible for his death.

The pathologist's report indicates that Tim was murdered first and then hung. It also now emerges that Cassidy himself might be gay. As far as the police are concerned this is a vital breakthrough, and DCI Bilborough orders Cassidy's arrest. Local feeling is running high, and the police car carrying Cassidy is mobbed as it makes it way into the station.

There is still very little forensic evidence linking Cassidy to the killing, and in the absence of a confession, Bilborough is forced to release him. The local community, stirred up by Tim'\s family are furious at this, and Cassidy's flat comes under attack. Cassidy is taken by Fitz and DS Beck to a secret hotel location for his own protection.

Fitz's home life remains as chaotic as ever. He is stuttering towards a reconciliation with Judith, but continues to flirt outrageously with Penhaligon, who, against her better judgement, remains attracted to Fitz. She is due two weeks leave at the end of the investigation, and invites a somewhat surprised Fitz to join her on holiday. There are going to be no easy one-night stands for Fitz. If he wants to be with her, then he will have to leave his family.

Back in the hotel, it has become a matter of professional pride for Fitz to get Cassidy to confess. Fitz is sure he is guilty, and he can't bear the idea that someone else could have the intellect or emotional strength to withstand him. After a series of psychologically bruising exchanges, Cassidy does confess, and he is taken back to the police station to be charged.

Beck claims the credit, but when Fitz goes to visit Cassidy for one last time in the cells, he realizes that the confession is false. Fitz rushes to Bilborough to try to persuade him to release Cassidy, but Bilborough has already called a press conference to announce the arrest, and doesn't want to lose face by calling it off. Both Fitz and Bilborough have to live with the knowledge that they are partially responsible for sending an innocent man to prison.

Back home Fitz looks out of the window at his wife and children as he packs his suitcase. Penhaligon waits alone under the airport departure board. Fitz joins his family in the garden; the family ties were just too great, and Penhaligon flies off alone.

SERIES TWO
TO BE A SOMEBODY

A local welder, Albie Kinsella, is seen at his father's funeral. Later on he goes into his local newsagent and tries to buy a box of tea-bags and a newspaper; he doesn't have quite enough money, and the Asian owner refuses to let him take the goods and come back later with the few extra pence. Albie goes home furious, and shaves his head. He then picks up his father's old bayonet, and returns to the shop and kills the owner.

The police are convinced that the murder has all the hallmarks of a racist attack. They make raids on the premises of all known National Front sympathizers, but fail to make any headway with the investigation.

Fitz meanwhile is putting his feet up at home. Neither he

nor DCI Bilborough are prepared to talk to one another following the Cassidy case, and Bilborough has enlisted the help
of another psychologist called Dr Nolan. Fitz is still trying to
stabilize his domestic situation with Judith and his children,
but he still can't quite come to terms with his jealousy over
Judith's affair, and things being to fall apart again when he
wins and loses a fortune at the casino and forgets his son,
Mark's, birthday. Overcome with depression, guilt and anxiety, Fitz winds up in hospital with a suspected heart attack.
Judith then leaves with Katie for the second time, and Fitz
tries desperately to patch up his relationship with Penhaligon,
who still hasn't forgiven him for jilting her at the airport.

Dr Nolan goes public with the profile of the killer as a
mindless, white, working-class thug.

This so enrages Albie, that after sitting in on one of Nolan's
lectures, he walks back with him to his office and murders
him.

Albie then turns his attention onto a woman journalist
working for The Sun, who only escapes becoming his third
victim by a lucky escape.

Fitz manages to persuade Penhaligon that Nolan's profile of
the killer is completely wrong, and this together with The Sun
journalist's description, helps to focus the investigation, and
DS Beck visits Albie as part of the enquiry. He asks Albie
about his newly shaved head, but is satisfied when Albie tells
him that he is undergoing chemotherapy and shows him an
appointment card for the cancer clinic at the local hospital.
The card in fact belonged to Albie's dad.

Albie decides to target DCI Bilborough. He follows
Bilborough's family to a local supermarket, where he molests
his wife. Concerned for his wife and baby, Bilborough com-

pletely forgets his professional training, and gives chase to Albie alone. He follows him through some narrow alleys back to Albie's house, where he is taken by surprise is knifed in the chest. As he lies bleeding outside the front door, he radios back to base with an exact location and description. Beck is mortified because he realizes that the killer is the man whom he had let go. Bilborough dies on the pavement as the police and ambulance turn up.

Despite early friction with DCI Wise, Bilborough's replacement, Fitz is back on the team, and he soon begins to understand Albie's motives. Albie and his Dad had been at Hillsborough on the day when 97 football fans were crushed to death, and he has still not forgiven the police for their handling of the situation nor The Sun for their reporting of it. Albie is now on the run, and we see him making a bomb in a shed.

Fitz realises that Albie's mission is to kill 97 people as revenge for Hillsborough, and suspects that he will turn up at the Manchester United v Liverpool football game. The police keep a close watch on the Liverpool supporters, but there is no sign of him. Too late, Fitz guesses that Albie will have bought a ticket off a home team supporter and by the time they search the United fans Albie has already been thrown out of the ground for causing trouble.

A chase ensues, and Albie is run to ground in the shed on his father's allotment. Under heavy pressure from Fitz, Albie admits his crimes. A letterbomb explodes in the offices of The Sun.

THE BIG CRUNCH

Lay preacher and school master Kenneth Trant is secretly photographed by his sister-in-law Norma as he makes love to Joanne - a teenaged pupil at his school, and a member of the strange fundamentalist sect which he leads.

Very different, but equally serious domestic troubles are looming again for Fitz. Judith is intent on a straight down-the-line division on the family and the family's assets. She puts the house on the market, leaving Fitz and Mark to fend for themselves. In response to these new emotional traumas Fitz starts to spend more and more time with DS Penhaligon, and an affair begins.

Meanwhile Kenneth's wife, Virginia, is presented with Norma's evidence of her husbands' adultery, and together they decide to protect Kenneth and the sect from any potential slur. In their minds Joanne becomes the seductress rather than the victim, and they decide to punish her for it. Aided by Kenneth, and his brother Michael, a not-so-willing accomplice, they invite Joanne to their home where they strip her, daub her boy with weird religious markings and torture her as part of a perverse ritual.

Assuming she is dead they instruct Dean, a simple young Bible study student at the sect, to dump a box containing Joanne's body into a baler machine at Michael's factory. But Dean decides to open the box, and finding Joanne - a girl whom he's always been fond of - still conscious, flees the scene in terror, torn between his loyalty to Joanne and the sect. A dazed Joanne emerges from the factory and disappears into the night.

After an extensive search she's picked up by the police, and Fitz set to work untangling her confused ramblings in an attempt to establish the identity of what he wrongly assumes at this stage is the single attacker who brought her to this strange fate.

After a while, Fitz discovers her involvement in the cult and begins to question various members. However he is met with a wall of silent. Everyone is either too loyal to the sect or too terrified to speak out. Even Joanne's schoolfriends in the sect - some of whom have also been abused by Kenneth - refuse to say a word against him.

After finding religious insignia in Dean's flat that are similar to those on Joanne's body, Dean is taken into police custody, where torn apart by guilt for his minor role in Joanne's torture and unable to break his silence, he hangs himself in the cells.

Eventually Fitz's persistence pays off; he pressurises Michael into talking out, and in a showdown in the cult's church, Kenneth is shown up for what he is as, one by one, the cult members turn their back on him.

Men Should Weep

Floyd is a young black man employed as a mini-cab driver. He is also a serial rapist, and after raping a work-mate's wife, he then turns up at a police reconstruction of one of his earlier attacks.

None of his victims has been able to provide an accurate description of their attacker, as he has always worn a balaclava and gone to great lengths to avoid leaving any means of identification, and the police investigation proceeds slowly. At this stage, they are not even certain how many rapes have been committed since some women are reluctant to report attacks.

DS Penhaligon is raped on a stairwell outside a block of

flats, and, because the modus operandi is so similar to the other assaults, the police believe that the same attacker is responsible. Unsurprisingly, Penhaligon is badly shaken by her ordeal, and she begins to distrust and feel alienated from all her male colleagues - including Fitz. At the same time Fitz's home life is thrown into even deeper confusion, when Judith returns home and announces that she is pregnant.

As the investigation continues, Fitz appears on a radio chat show to discuss the growing number of rapes. Floyd can't resist ringing in. He is arrogant enough to believe that he is untouchable, and curious to discover what progress the police are making. Without revealing his identity, he starts to niggle Fitz about how little he knows. At one stage, Floyd asks Fitz what the best method of avoiding detection is, and Fitz, letting his anger get the better of his judgement, suggests that he ought to kill his next victim ...... advice that Floyd then proceeds to follow.

It gradually emerges that the rapist is black, and this along with other crucial evidence, leads to Floyd's arrest. During the course of the interrogation, Fitz begins to unravel Floyd's motivation. He is half white, half Afro-Caribbean, and has always felt uncomfortable in his own skin. As a child he even dipped his leg in acid to try and remove the colouring. His rapes are a way of expressing both his anger at his situation, and against white women whom he believes have never accepted him.

In the meantime, Penhaligon has realized that Floyd was not the man who raped her. Sitting next to DS Beck in the police station she is overcome by the same smell of after-shave that has remained locked in her subconscious since the rape. She tells DCI Wise her suspicions about Beck. Wise tries to be impartial, pointing out the difficulties of obtaining evidence and the damage such an accusation, if unproven, could do to both her's and Beck's career. Penhaligon is far from happy about this, and retreats further into her private world. She wants revenge, and at the moment she doesn't care what she has to do to get it. Her relationship with Fitz is deteriorating rapidly, and, in one memorable scene, she tries to make him feel as helpless as she felt when she was raped, by driving extremely fast and dangerously through the city.

Floyd is on the verge of confessing to Fitz, when his lawyer intervenes and obtains his release because the evidence against him is purely circumstantial. Floyd emerges more disturbed than ever from the questioning, determined to exact his own violent revenge. The police follow him, expecting him to strike again, but lose him. They concentrate on protecting all his previous victims, and it is only at the last minute that they realize one crucial person has been overlooked.

Floyd has gone to Fitz's house, where he is planning to kill Judith. Fitz and the police appear just in time, and Floyd is overcome after a desperate fight.

On the other side of town, Penhaligon is lying in wait for DS Beck at his home. She surprises him, and threatens him with a gun. She is too professional to kill him, but she wants him to know what rape feels like. Calmly, she orders him to open his mouth, and in a moment of symbolic forced penetration, places the gun barrel inside.

has a practical usage. It has created extra categories apart from 'organised' and 'disorganised' by which to interpret patterns of crime, and in one famous case it helped the police to solve a series of ten rapes in the Midlands in 1988. Although there was no direct forensic evidence to connect the assaults, there were sufficient similarities for the police to believe that all the rapes had been committed by the same person. All the victims were women students in rented accommodation who were attacked while sleeping alone, and on each occasion the assailant was black. What is more, apart from on the first occasion which might just have been an experiment and on the sixth when he was disturbed, the attacker always asked the victim for help in achieving penetration.

Professor Canter was called into the investigation in 1989. He, too, initially assumed that the rapes had been committed by the same person, but as he studied the evidence it began to dawn on him that there might be two attackers involved. While consistently asking for help with penetration might seem damning evidence of just one assailant, there were no statistics to prove it. If asking for such help was quite common during a rape, then it would be no pointer to anyone in particular. However, while the range of sexual activities and levels of violence might suggest an attacker that was growing in confidence, evidence from solved cases suggested that a rapist who reassured and fondled his victims was unlikely to be capable of a masked, violent attack.

Before Professor Canter had fully determined whether two offenders were involved, forensic scientists settled the matter for him by detecting two different strands of DNA in samples left behind by the attackers. However, there was still the small matter of identifying the assailants. Canter and his team began to analyze the crimes in still greater behavioural detail, and were able to attribute each crime to a particular attacker. Those of the rapist who saw his victims as people were labelled the work of the 'Wimp', and those of the rapist who saw his victims as objects they called the work of 'Macho Man'. Working on expected life and behaviour patterns of each type of rapist, and drawing a circle around each set of rapes, Canter drew up a profile of the attackers and predicted where they might live. In June 1989 two men were arrested and later received long prison sentences for their part in the rapes. Both conformed to the profile that Professor Canter had drawn up, and lived within the area predicted.

Offender profiling has by no means been one man's preserve in this country. Dr Paul Britton has also contributed significantly to some prominent police investigations. He produced a stunningly accurate portrait of Michael Sams after the murder of Julie Dart. Sams, he said, would be in his late 40s to early 50s, would be familiar with electric tools and machinery though not a senior employee in an organisation, would make contact with the police, and would re-offend. Britton was right in all these predictions, but unfortunately Sams was not caught until after Stephanie Slater had been abducted and imprisoned. He helped to negotiate Stephanie's release, and was on hand at Sams' trial to advise the prosecution counsel. It was also Paul Britton's advice that the police look for an ex-policeman in the baby foods contamination enquiry, that resulted in the conviction of Detective Sergeant Rodney Whitchelo.

Offender profiling has justifiably grabbed the public's attention: while it is true that most murders and rapes are solved by more conventional police work, forensic psychology has helped to crack some of the most seemingly impenetrable cases. Yet it is important to remember that it is very early days for criminal psychology, and there are still some crucial moral and scientific questions for forensic psychology to answer. It has been suggested that the publication of details on profiling will enable certain criminals to second guess the police by acting in an unpredictable way. This seems a relatively minor worry; psychology is based on studies of behaviour and thought patterns, and it is as improbable for a criminal to act out of character as it would be for you and I.

More worrying is that suspects may be arrested and brought in for questioning with no corroborative evidence merely because they fit a profile; likewise, if the suspect is guilty, but refuses to confess, the police would have to let him go, and there is a known correlation between offenders moving up to murder after their release from custody. In such circumstances should a suspect be brought in for questioning? If he isn't might he not re-offend anyway?

Despite the efforts of Robert Ressler and David Canter, offender profiling is still far from being an exact science. Indeed, one gender has so far been largely ignored. Most of the modern research has been focused on men, because it was always widely held that women don't become serial killers. Recent evidence contradicts this somewhat. Christopher Missen, a postgraduate student in Professor Canter's own department has compiled an exhaustive list of British serial killers over the last one hundred years. There have been 110 in all, of which 20 have been women.

There is still a great deal to be discovered and understood about how serial killers think and behave before offender profiling becomes truly scientific, and so insight and intuition continues to be an important part of the criminal psychologist's armoury. As Ian Stephen says: 'Whenever a new murder is announced on the radio or TV, I get a gut feeling about it. Just by listening to a few details, I can almost invariably tell whether it is a domestic incident, a gangland killing, or a serial killing, and make predictions in my head about what type of person the police should be looking for.' Whether profiling can ever become wholly scientific remains to be seen, but there will certainly be one person who will be delighted if it never does. Can you imagine Fitz tied to a computer screen?